A.D. Moddie, an ex-I.A.S. officer, has served as the Director of Hindustan Lever Ltd. from 1966-76. He has worked as a senior consultant to the German Government and has been Chairman of Himalayan Eco-development Association of Scientists and Professionals. He has authored four books and has contributed articles on political and economic affairs to newspapers.

LEADERS OF STRAW: INDIA'S FIRST 50 YEARS

A.D. Moddie

HarperCollins *Publishers* India

HarperCollins *Publishers* India Pvt Ltd
7/16 Ansari Road, Daryaganj, New Delhi 110 002

Published 1997 by
HarperCollins *Publishers* India

ISBN 81-7223-277-2

Cover design by Bitten Nails

Typeset by
Megatechnics
19A, Ansari Road
New Delhi 110 002

Printed in India by
Gopsons Papers Ltd
A-28, Sector IX
Noida 201 301

Dedication

This short book is dedicated to the people of India, its Defence Services, and specially the next generation, by one who was of the generation of Nehru's promised 'tryst with destiny' at midnight on 15th August 1947. That generation failed the hopes of a new, credulous nation, a democracy so hard in the making. The prime responsibility for that was with what passed for leadership after Sardar Patel, men and women of straw, who have appropriately imaged themselves in cardboard cutouts — larger than life, far smaller than their roles — when the images of earlier leaders were in metal or stone. Dedicated to the people, this book is commended to the political, bureaucratic, technocratic, military and intellectual ruling classes, who have not governed. To rule and not to govern is to be where you should not be. That is the core problem of the new democracy. It is too credulous, too trusting of the Nehru generation of leaders, too confused about the role of state, market, international affairs, and themselves, in a feudal past culture of an omniscient but corrupt *sirkar*. The people have been both accomplice and victim in what has happened, but there is a basic decency in the Indian people, which needs good exemplary leadership more than anything else and a no-nonsense attitude towards the rulers who misgovern and mismanage, whatever their caste or creed. They have belied the claim to be trusted representatives of the people. They have hijacked the polity and the economy. And they are ripe for the dustbin of history.

Contents

Foreword

To answer the question posed by the former Prime Minister — What went wrong in the fifty years we have been masters of our fate — would comfortably fill as many volumes as the current Encyclopaedia Brittanica! Despite the daunting nature of this task, the author, Mr. A.D. Moddie, manages to give an insightful overview in response to Mr. Deve Gowda's rhetorical question within the compass of this small book — *Leaders of Straw : India's first fifty years*.

This is a book which will leave the reader in a pessimistic frame of mind — for the most fundamental of reasons. What did our country lack? And how profligate were we in squandering our golden opportunities and plentiful resources? Self-seeking politicians, antiquated notions of socialism, myriad catch words and hollow phrases, unhealthy protection of industry, keeping out market forces of competition, the marvellous ploy of blaming 'the foreign hand' for almost any problem, resorting to populist measures such as nationalizing banks which promoted those loan mela dramas, abolishing privy purses — all contributed in generous measure to keeping the economy in chains and India firmly part of the fourth world.

Mr. Moddie has given the reader many, very telling facts and figures in several areas of the economy and of urban and rural life, which confront us with the harsh reality of how little we have progressed and achieved. That fifty years down the independence road, shamefully a large mass of our people live below the poverty line without the barest of basic amenities in conditions of appalling degradation, must give us pause for thought. The government's official figure of those living below the poverty line is presently 36 per cent of our population — a very large number considering we are 900 million strong. The reader will realize how misleading this figure is, when he sees that it is based merely on caloric sustenance levels in the rural and urban areas translated into 1992-93 rupee terms. Were one to factor in the cache of essentials such as shelter, clothing, water, electricity, education, the fictitious 36 per cent figure would escalate sharply.

Added to this depressing scene is the lasting environmental degradation and damage that we have permitted to be inflicted upon us for what the author has termed 'local profit' by 'politicians of opportunities'. It is of small moment to our myopic politicians and corrupt bureaucrats that our environmental future has thus been largely mortgaged. We have not inherited the earth from our forefathers; we have borrowed it from our children.

Perhaps the single largest factor contributing to what has gone wrong has been an endemic and all pervasive corruption. Mr. Moddie retails this succinctly. He rightly analyzes and concludes that the 'culture of *sirkar*' originating in the licence and permit raj of old, where the political presence is strongly felt — combined with thin regard for accountability, are responsible for this phenomenon. One has only to glance at the day's papers to see how widespread and corrosive corruption is — scams and scandals a-plenty — punctuated by amnesty schemes for tax dodgers, are our daily headlines. The lessons from the Indian experience summed up by the author are important imperatives for all to study and ponder over.

Happily, Mr. Moddie does not leave the topic of his book, which would be the cause for much gloom, without constructive suggestions put together in the form of an agenda for the future. This outlines what we can do to rise, phoenix-like, from the ashes of the past. Provided, I might add, we have the political will and courage to do so (talent and enterprise we have in generous measure), coupled with a firm resolve to limit our alarmingly burgeoning population which effectively negates advance.

The events commented upon in the postscript to the book, which deal with the most significant developments of this year, will not inspire any confidence or hope in the reader. Political shenanigans and manoeuvring for power have taken precedence over the needs of India for a stable, strong government and economy.

Mr. Moddie ends his very readable book by surveying the little we have achieved in 50 years of Independence and with an apt quotation from Shakespeare. Let me add mine to his — also from Shakespeare —

But yet the pity of it Iago!
O Iago, the pity of it, — Iago.

15th April 1997 — Nani A. Palkhivala

Introduction

But man, proud man,
Dress'd in a little brief
authority,
Most ignorant of what he's
most assured,
His glassy essence, like an
angry ape,
Plays such fantastic tricks
before high heaven,
As makes the angles weep.

— **William Shakespeare.**
Measure for Measure.

In India's fiftieth year of Independence the former Prime Minister, Shri H.D. Deve Gowda, in a revival meeting of India's dormant Planning Commission asked: 'What has gone wrong and where?' He asked the Planning Commission to do some soul-searching. Neither a Prime Minister nor a Planning Commission can be expected to be soul-searching saints. They have been participants in the game of what went wrong. In their official capacities, politicians and bureaucrats do not care even to define what has gone wrong, apart from elaborating and curing it. But it is something for the highest political product of the times, now at the top of the heap, to raise this simple question so directly. In a way, it should be a question addressed to the whole nation from the ramparts of the Red Fort on 15th August, fifty years after Nehru spoke about his 'tryst with destiny' for himself and for 'midnight's children'.

I try to address myself to that question from my early personal intimations, 1940 to 1970, from Churchill's famous 'men of straw' prognostications plagiarised from Nostradamus, to this fiftieth year of mixed disillusionment and hope, focusing mainly on the economy and the polity. That Churchill-Nostradamus forecast — which we disliked and dismissed at the time as the ranting of a bygone imperialist — is today an amazingly true forecast of India's vernacularised political *leaderi,* not leadership, especially after Lal Bahadur Shastri. It is worth recalling that forecast :

'Power will go into the hands of rascals, rogues, freebooters (and now to use the press idiom, scamsters)... These are the men of straw, of whom no trace will be found after a few years. (They are still at the top of the heap after fifty years). They will be fighting among themselves, and India will be lost in political squabbles'. Unfortunately, that past forecast 'of whom no trace will be found' after fifty years has not yet materialised. The men and women of straw and cardboard are very much on top of the heap. India is just waking up to the enormity of the rascality, roguery and freebooting.

Some of us may ask, why Nostradamus and why Churchill? The answer is simple. None of us could forecast the shape of things to come before 1969 and none of us have dared to answer the question, 'What went wrong?' publicly in clear terms, post-1969.

In 1982, in his acceptance speech of the Magsaysay Award, Arun Shourie, a one-time press crusader, said with much political wisdom :

> The evil of the rulers will persist so long as we partake of it, so long as we lend ourselves as instruments for its execution, so long as we assist it by putting up with it, by doing nothing to end it... We have partaken of it, we have lent ourselves as instruments, we have assisted it by putting up with it, especially as bureaucrats, businessmen, contractors, educators, professionals, and voters. We have put ministers on pedestals, and deified political office. We have allowed ourselves to be duped by power-mongers too long. So the evil of the rulers has persisted. The people of India have been both accomplices and victims of what went wrong.

Let us try and analyse this masquerading *leaderi* and the role of the people of India, both as accomplices and as victims. Before I say what I wish to say, may I quote V.S. Naipaul to meet the usual allegation of Indians self-flagellating themselves? When, in 1993 he was being interviewed by L.K. Sharma in London in his reference to 'upheavals' and 'change', he said, 'I see even your feeling of despair as creative', and 'major countries have to regenerate themselves'. It is in that spirit to help seek creative regeneration that I pen these hard lines. I also subscribe to Naipaul's view that we should not 'pine for simple old days', nor should we look to charismatic leaders for redemption, to take the burden from our shoulders. Only peasant and tribal cultures need such leaders, not modernised ones with a large educated class. He added, 'when you have this large body of educated people, you can't have those charismatic leaders.' It is to this large body of educated readers, Pascal's 'thinking reeds', that I address this book for the next fifty years of the Republic of India. A higher sense of citizenship, in small and big ways, is the new starting point for a better 'tryst with destiny'. We need a strong citizenship of millions, and leaders of substance and spirit, not straw and *sauda* (trade).

I should conclude this Introduction by clarifying that this book is confined to answering former Prime Minister Deve Gowda's question, 'What went wrong?' The major lessons of India's first fifty years are there. So what may have gone right, the positive achievements are excluded. For the record, atleast let us remind ourselves of that more positive side. It is not insignificant. Beginning with adult franchise and the political maturing of the Indian electorate after the Emergency, the record stretches to the Green Revolution and food self-sufficiency in an earlier land of famines, to the independent role of the higher judiciary, to new institutions like the Indian Institutes of Management and Indian Institutes of Technology, the new steel-frame of development, to the software cradle of Bangalore, the growing missile programme, and the far better condition of about two-thirds of India's children than in 1947. But these are far outdone by the worsening failures of the whole body of a revenue-hungry ineffective government, the cancer of corruption and lawlessness, and the undermining of the morale of a people, who trusted their leaders too much for their own good and for a strong democracy.

Early Intimations

Each succeeding day is the Scholar of that which went before it.

— Publius Syrus

I am not one of the 'midnight's children'. I grew up as a boy in the evening of the British Indian empire, and as a young man after the dawn of Independence. Like millions of Indians then, I spent hours at mass meetings listening to the powerful orations of Subhas Chandra Bose in Shillong, to the classical Urdu diction of Maulana Azad and the halting speeches of Nehru in Allahabad. There, in the heart of the national movement, I was once moved by the power of a strong bare-bodied Gandhi in taming a restless Indian crowd with a quiet intonation of '*Shanti, Shanti, Shanti*'. And the crowd was silenced. I imbibed a quiet patriotism, like youth today sipping cola from a straw, casually. I had read of patriotism being the last resort of scoundrels. In India it has been the first. The fervour of the revolutionary, of the freedom-fighter was not for me; not even that breeding ground of future politicians of repute and disrepute, the Allahabad University Students' Union. I was a serious student of history — that mirror of leaders of many peoples over the centuries.

I reflected on both the macro turbulence around me, and the micro events of University life. Of the macro political leaders, only Gandhi seemed to me to be a man of real character, a leader of the spirit in tough times. Most seemed like agitated word processors, glorified into leaders by the patriotic emotion of an emotional people in emotional times. The leaders of the University union seemed to me like rascally opportunists with no spine, not beyond sequestering Student Union funds. They were the future 'men of straw' and *sauda* (trade). One of them became a well-known Chief Minister of Uttar Pradesh. When, thirty years later, I called on him in that post to tell him frankly that his 'raids' on the trade and such antics were doing the people more harm than good, that it was driving even the scarce essential commodities into the black market, his nonchalant answer was, 'Moddie Sahib, *Yeh to dikhane ke liye karna parta*!' After that I never forgot that politics was a theatre, and that the acts and gestures of politicians were '*dikhane ke liye*', an empty show to fool the public. This was real life political sociology.

During 1940 and 1942, at the Allahabad University I saw three portents of the future. The first was Hindu-Muslim communalism, a portent of the Partition of India. It was particularly blatant on the Muslim side. The Muslim hostel in the University seemed to be a separate nucleus of the future Pakistan, and many of its alumni ended up there.

They were a distinct group then, a kind of product of the separate electorates of the Thirties, in dress, language, mind-frame and style. I don't remember one Azad, one nationalist Muslim among them. There may have been, but like me they must have been quiet and invisible. I sensed this separateness, a little premonition of Pakistan, in my amusing experiences as a member of the University Cricket Team. Nine of the eleven players were Muslims. I, a Parsi, was adopted as 'Moddie Mia'. That left one Rajasthani Hindu, a kind of stepney player. When the rest of India produced so many Hindu cricketers, I cannot explain the disproportion between Muslim and Hindu players, except as communal exclusiveness. The adoption of 'Moddie Mia' isolated the only Hindu. We were beaten by both Benares Hindu University and Aligarh Muslim University. But the match against Benares seemed to have a competitive verve about it, whilst the defeat at the hands of Aligarh was taken humbly as from a superior kindred power. In later years, I had little doubt of Aligarh being a cultural and religious seedbed of Pakistan. It exuded Muslim separatism proudly.

Whilst my father, in a distant district of Bengal, was building Hindu temples and Muslim *Idgahs* to maintain a peaceful balance between the communities, I was experiencing this separateness, this communal virus in the Indian society for the first time, a premonition of the horrible three-day Calcutta killings which I saw in shame with my own eyes in 1946, and the devastating disruption of the division of India in 1947. As a one-time historian, this problem still intrigues me. How did we come from Akbar's, the Mughal-Rajput's composite culture, as it was called, to the harsh fanaticism of a puritan Muslim like Aurangzeb, and the equally harsh political fanaticism of a Westernised, dandy Muslim like Jinnah? But then I was only sensing the germs of hostility in the coming communal calamities of the future, pre- and post-1947.

My second observation among the ways of the University students was the wider suppressed sexuality and violence, which went together. It was, and has continued to be expressed, through the institutionalised ragging of freshers. Ostensibly, it was a kind of bullying of a stupid kind, in which the older students exercised their power over 'freshers', and made them sing or dance or do some ridiculous performance. But there was a thin, uncertain psychological line, which could be crossed over into vulgarity. I had heard about some past incidents where this had happened and made it known that we would go through the fun part of the performance, but if the line of decency was crossed we would fight. It was not crossed. Most Indian students at that time had no opportunity for decent social mixing between the sexes, so repressed sex seethed through hungry eyes, and expressed itself in vulgar jokes and vulgar language; sometimes in subtle Urdu. Here were indications of a deep psycho-social malaise, which in the coming decades manifested in social disorder, in a cruel, unequal relationship with women, perhaps the worst evil of India and with frequent reports of rapes from all sections of Indian society, urban and rural. I have read that rape is as much an urge to violence, as to sex. That can of worms has never quite been opened to conservative, face-saving Indian society. I have wondered whether one of the reasons of widespread violence in India has its roots there. It has taken fifty years of a democratic, socialist India to allow a few women to emerge as Panchayti Raj leaders; and then only with the consent of their husbands and families. The inequality between man and woman in our society is the worst and most widespread of human inequalities, the single major impediment to human development in education and health and progress, upon which all other development is based. Our post-1947 leaders, even women leaders, have ignored this.

The third insight was into the contrast between the earlier British-time upper-class Indian, and the new generation of my time coming out of India's dark social hinterland. This contrast was exemplified, for example, between Prof. Amarnath Jha, a high level, respected Vice-Chancellor, a teacher of English, who quoted from Shakespeare, even though a little pompously; and the future *leaderi* in the University union. Amarnath Jha, whatever he was, symbolised quality, excellence and character. The men from the dark social hinterland emerged as office-bearers of the University Students' Union, excelling neither in studies nor in sports, but in political agitation, sometimes living off membership subscriptions, a style which later came to be called *leaderi*. Such men have spread in their millions all over the land post-1947, especially post-1970. They have been the political cancer of this country, its brazen plunderers, its massive corrupters, its underminers of good government and civic society. So here one saw a clear divide between the best products of an earlier generation of Indians, the products of the best in

Indian tradition and British education and government; and the new predators, the men of straw coming out of the woodwork of a political culture, of which Gandhi, Tagore, and Gokhale would have been ashamed.

In retrospect, I find it amazing how these early insights cast such long shadows, and led to far wider social and political repercussions. Others, like myself, have lived into times when 'elite' was a bad word in the illusions of an early, immature democracy talking of equalities, but still exhibiting feudal atavistic traits. I have no doubt of the value of a true elite in this and all past ages. Just as I have no doubt about the dangerous consequences of a non-elite *leaderi* who know not that they know not, and who are only a wider breed of parasites, ugly to behold, ridiculous in their pompousness, not conspicuous for integrity, decency or responsibility.

By the time I finished University, the Japanese had swept down the east coast of Asia in a military hurricane, had taken Singapore, invaded Burma, and were threatening India's eastern frontier. My home was in the east, in Bengal. I decided to join the army to defend that frontier. In the battle of the Arakan in 1944 we were outmanoeuvred, outgeneralled and routed by the Japanese. Later General Slim, our 14th Army Commander, steadily built up a strong defence to counter the attacks along the Manipur border. The Japanese push came as expected. There were fierce and bloody battles around Imphal and Kohima.

I come to the point of my story. I, in the uniform of a British-Indian Army officer, well-fed, well-clothed and armed, came face to face with some captured Indian

National Army (INA) prisoners of war. They were ill-fed on only rice-water. They had no uniforms, no arms; they were wrapped in torn tentage. I could not help but admire them. Perhaps they and I were equally justified in the positions we took, though theirs was in a more patriotic aura. But what was the reality behind that aura? We, in India were led to believe that the INA were Japanese comrades-in-arms, who came to free India under the leadership of the legendary Subhas Chandra Bose. In my admiration for these men I never questioned their integrity and their patriotism. But the reality was that they were not comrades-in-arms. No leader of men in modern war should commit men to battle in the way I found them. It was morally wrong and militarily demeaning. Yet this is what the Japanese did to them, treated them as unsoldierly public relations front-line cover for their own troops, ill-fed, clothed in rags, unarmed. I can only relate this small bit that I saw. What could one expect from those who slave-drove prisoners of war, including Indians, to construct the Malay Straits Railway, who failed to respect the Geneva Convention for prisoners of war, and who had, since 1931, brutalised Asian men and prostituted Asian women in the whole of East Asia.

After the Japanese surrender, the INA were feted as national heroes, despite the record of the Japanese. When senior officers of the INA were put on trial, Nehru, Bhulabhai Desai and the Congress party came to their defence. It was a dramatic trial, a show of patriotism under British law, which the Japanese would never have tolerated. I recall Nehru appearing for once in a black lawyer's gown, though the legal defence was left to the lawyer, Bhulabhai Desai. It seemed theatrical on Nehru's part. The trial blew over. Some of the senior officers joined the ranks of the Congress party and became ministers later. What happened to the thousands of the rank and file? Nehru and his government were persuaded by a British Commander-in-Chief, perhaps rightly, not to reinstate them in the Indian Army. They were forgotten. They went into oblivion. Was this a dramatic lesson in the politician's *'dikhane ke liye'* from Nehru himself? If not in the army, why could they not have been absorbed in the next five or ten years of the same Nehru's raj in the growing police forces of India, and in the growing civil government structure? The INA trial was made into a passing political show, a lesson for many such in future decades, like Republic Day parades, and like the Joint Parliamentary Committee's enquiry into the Bofors scandal, chaired by a Congress minister, who was later involved in the *Hawala* and Health Ministry scandals. It was another indication of the shape of things to come. But the nation was too euphoric then for rational thinking, too immature to assess its political leaders objectively.

These early intimations now go into my early years in the Indian Administrative Services (IAS). My fate was to be cross-posted to the Bihar cadre from the Bombay cadre. At the departmental examinations held in Patna in 1949, I witnessed massive cheating by officers of the IAS and provincial cadres, aided and abetted by official invigilators. These invigilators even cautioned the officer examinees before the arrival of the Member, Board of Revenue. Here was an eye-opening example of connivance in cheating in the new regime by officers themselves, in what we now look back to as the halcyon days of Nehru. The same officers were meant to implement the Indian Penal Code, the Criminal Procedure Code, and a host of regulatory legislations to regulate the lives of the Indian public with fairness and integrity, and according to law and regulation. Here was a shocking, brazen example of the widespread Indian phenomenon, official and non-official, of cheating and ambivalence. Here were the roots of the cheating by the official fathers themselves, and of examinations of the whole educational system, now criminalised by our politics. Here were the roots of massive 'systems failures' attested to by a rare, honest but evasive Finance Minister at the time of the Bank scam forty-five years later.

When I was in Muzaffarpur as an Assistant Magistrate, I experienced nothing of the earlier upbringing of the young Indian Civil Service (ICS) people by their District Magistrates (DM) in the days of 'The Guardians', pre-1947. My DM was a man who, in the course of decades, managed to rise in the same district from the junior most level of the bureaucracy. He never once spoke to me. I received no guidance. The days of training young civil servants on-the-job were over. The days of *pairvi* and *sifarish* were back, as in the days of the Nawabs and Rajas. The Chief Minister's closest friend and ally was from Muzaffarpur. He had no official position in the government, but he held court, and officers paid court to him. I neither knew of the ways of paying court, nor had the desire to do so. So I soon received my first independent charge in Madhubani, on the borders of Nepal, regarded then as a kind of Andamans or what used to be called 'a punishment posting'. Who said India had to wait twenty years to know of 'unconstitutional authority' in Sanjay Gandhi's time? 'Unconstitutional authority' has become a widespread phenomenon, the informal side of the Indian way of doing business, official or any other. We knew about it from 1949 among state politicians.

We have since known the massive transfer of hundreds of officers in the states, partly an exercise of arbitrary power, partly a political exercise of sifting the 'committed' (of Mrs. Gandhi fame) and the uncommitted (somebody else's man), and not least, as a widespread *sauda* in official postings, in which every post has a 'makings' price. There is no place that the politician's nose does not penetrate for money, whatever may be the consequences for good government and the people.

En route from Muzaffarpur to Madhubani in Bihar, I thought I should break journey at Darbhanga for a day to meet my Commissioner, a nice South Indian ICS gentleman of no particular distinction. He asked me when I was taking charge. When I told him it was the next Wednesday, he instructed me not to take charge on that day, but on the next Friday, despite government instructions. When I asked for the reason, he told me that Wednesday was inauspicious, whereas Friday was auspicious. So much in government is governed by the advice of astrologers, recently by the higher *avatar* of godmen from Mrs. Gandhi's Dhirendra Brahmachari trading in aircraft and arms factories, to P.V. Narasimha Rao's Chandraswami, alleged to be trading in every possible international racket, to humbler holy men who sit on *machans* and put a gentle foot on the heads of ministers to win elections and retain office; just to enable all of these to make 'sacrifices' for the poor of the country, in a secular technological Nehruvian model. A kind of sanctified democracy of rogues. This is another example of ambivalence.

Afterwrds, I went to meet my DM (also stationed in Darbhanga), not in the IAS, but a good honest officer of the pre-1947 regime. He cautioned me that I was walking into a dangerous situation with my new charge. My visions of 'The Guardians' took a body blow when he unfolded to me how the Deputy Inspector General, CID, of the State of Bihar had committed an armed dacoity with his own men on a Mahant in my sub-division, as the DIG and his son, who had been married to the Mahant's daughter, were impatient to grab the lands and property of the Mahant, before his normal demise. He added that documentary evidence of it was in his office safe, to which he pointed. We have long since heard of police excesses, 'encounters', *zulum*, the blinding of Bhagalpur prisoners, and the condemning of the police by a judge as 'criminals in uniform'; but the perpetration of an armed dacoity by a senior police officer of the rank of DIG, CID in 1949, in the halcyon days of the Nehru raj was a loud ringing of Nostradamus' bell for a young officer assuming his first charge. It was the ringing in of the law of the *lathi*, of '*jis ki lathi uski bhains*'. I also knew of the grabbing of lands by the most distinguished families in Bihar, aided and abetted by the police, preventing defensive action by the immediate resort to *S. 144 Cr. PC*, and then futile protracted proceedings in the courts was the only option left to the weaker victims. No wonder three land reform bills in Bihar remained ineffective. No wonder Bihar is what it has since become, India's Central African state.

I had to tackle three years of the Kosi's devastating floods in Madhubani, three years in which I saw our poor marginal people, men, women and children, lying helplessly on damp floors, malaria-ridden, fevered, under-nourished bodies, with little or no relief, passive remnants of life. I initiated out-board motors on country boats to carry relief faster to the stranded thousands hit by extensive floods, and spread over hundreds of square miles. It was the worst human suffering I had seen since the Bengal famine. Not a single minister of Bihar, all virtuous, khadi-clad freedom fighters till yesterday, the heirs of Gandhi, cared to make a single visit in all those three years. One day I heard the Chief Minister was coming. On the flight over the Kosi flooded areas he asked me, 'When the Prime Minister comes, what shall I say?' The cat was out of the bag. The real reason of his visit was revealed as clear as daylight. If it were not for the news of the Prime Minister's visit to my sub-division, the great *neta* would not have interrupted his feasting on chicken and *sandesh*, which he devoured despite diabetes and flatulence, amidst the comfort of Patna, the state's capital. I recalled that the first distinguished person to be concerned with the devastating annual Kosi floods only five years earlier, was none other than the British Viceroy Lord Wavell, from whom these same *netas* were supposed to have delivered us into freedom and a better life. Who was the better 'Guardian', that British Viceroy or this Indian Chief Minister, in the context of the Kosi's victims?

When I was in the midst of Kosi relief work in Madhepur, the news broke of Sardar Patel's death. I thought the best way of paying our respects to this great and respected leader was to carry on the day's good work for those afflicted thousands. To my surprise, the local khadi-clad *netas* insisted on commemorating by a holiday and a cessation of relief work. Here, I realised, was the seed of the new post-1947 Indian work ethic. Every excuse, festival or death was a good enough reason for a holiday and a cessation of work from grass roots to our august Parliament. The deaths of the far lesser men than the Sardar continues to provide reasons for Parliamentary holidays, at the countable expense of lakhs of rupees per day, and the unaccountable cost of urgent legislative work of the nation.

Mention of Sardar Patel leads me to an amusing side-light on our informal ways of relating with others, especially those in power or authority; ways which go back to Chanakya. I realised I was a bit of an oddity in Madhubani, because the gentry could not fix the caste to which I belonged. Going back to the days of *Arthashastra* when ruler and ruled tried to fix each other by knowing each others' 'weaknesses', they seemed to find my 'weakness' was not in the usual Omar Khayyam fields of wine, women and song, but in mountains. They seemed nonplussed as to how to fix me in that area, that too in the middle of the flat Gangetic plain. The town gentry had heard from servant gossip that my wife and I spoke Gujarati at home. So this clever gentry immediately jumped to the conclusion that I was 'Sardar Patel's man' presumbaly planted in Bihar to keep an eye on the notorious machinations of the Bhumihar and Rajput caste politics. This amusing assumption was fortified one day when one of the gentry, a leading doctor of the town said, 'May I ask you, Mr. Moddie, what is your caste?' At last the teasing question had surfaced. In fun I told him that I was a Surat Brahmin, and like Maithil Brahmins I too wore a sacred thread, what we Parsis call the *Kusti*.

Thereafter, I was made, into a combination of 'Sardar Patel's man' and a respectable Brahmin in highly legitimised authority. Far from this being an isolated humorous story of one individual, both aspects of it, being 'the man' of a powerful personage and being a Brahmin in a caste-ridden society, were strong behaviour traits in our society, especially in the power structure from district to Delhi. In India one cannot be one's own man. That is absurd. In a caste hierarchy of power, where each has superiors to scrape to and inferiors to bully and exploit, the behaviour of autonomous institutions seems foreign, and the behaviour of autonomous individuals intolerable. This is somewhat troublesome when the specious outer aspiration is for a secular democracy of equals. Between the outer ideological aspiration, and the inner cultural reality, lie many problems not least those of good government between an autonomous, though loyal permanent executive brought up in the non-institutional environment of the joint family with the *karta* as the recognised head; of the all pervasive and deep caste hierarchy, of the *zamindar*-tenant and *jajmani* relationship of patron and client; capped by the equally traditional, dominant 'culture of the *sirkar*'. So forty years down the road, after a Constitution for law and egalitarianism, the Mandal bomb broke upon the traditional governing machines of India. In those early years, most of us lived in the innocent belief that modernisation would weaken these traditional ways, especially caste. Now caste is stronger than ever in my lifetime. Another foreboding. The heart of our modernisation process does not lie with only economic policies, but in our functioning styles. In that respect, our politicians and our leaders in all walks of life, still betray the behaviour traits of a feudal India, and we have largely remained backward isolates in a changing world, as will be seen in later chapters.

Let me present another little cameo of my frontier days. When the Nepal Independence movement of the emigre 'C' class Ranas in India against the 'A' and 'B' Class Rana regime in Nepal was under way; on grounds of maintaining law and order in a dacoit infested frontier, we were given authority to penetrate Nepal up to 50 miles. For me this was a youthful adventure, unmindful of the sensitivities of a breach of international law against a neighbouring state. That should have been more appropriately a concern of the Prime Minister, who was also the Foreign Minister. When I arrived at the office of my opposite number, the *Bada Hakim* of the district, over tea he expressed his natural displeasure, almost hostility. He said, 'All this (meaning the so-called Independence movement) was no one's *bahaduri* (bravery), this was Chandu's *bahaduri*.' By Chandu he meant Chandeshwar Prasad Singh, a distinguished Bihari, then our ambassador in Kathmandu who, it was widely alleged, had engineered the change of regime. This was a very dubious machination in the name of a democratic regime. Was this a touch of India's later foreign policy in the region with smaller powers? Whether it was or not, it certainly followed decades of suspicion against India's Big Brother attitude, a hatred of its arrogance, culminating in that not-so-attractive image of a bully with small neighbouring states, and a *Jagatguru* on international platforms. The inescapable ambivalence again. For the next forty years, India ignored its Asian neighbours, and tried to play *Jagatguru* with larger Western powers, losing out on both fronts, a basically flawed policy which took four decades and the Asian-Pacific resurgence to discover.

Soon I was transferred to the state headquarters as Textile Controller of the state. The circumstances of the transfer provide yet another insight in Nehru's days of the shape of things to come. I was trekking on holiday in the Satopanth area in Garhwal. En route to the Valley of Flowers, I received a telegram at Badrinath to report to the Supply department immediately. Despite my disappointment, I returned and reported to the Secretary, Supply, who, to my surprise, asked me why I had rushed back. Only later I discovered the true reason. The previous Textile Controller was known to have been collecting large funds from the textile trade, then under controls. But the offence was not looked upon as corruption. His fault was that he was collecting money for his minister, the leader of the rival faction of Rajputs, in the same Congress government with a rival Bhumihar Chief Minister. The Chief Minister insisted on his immediate removal. I was chosen as a safe substitute.

In view of the subsequent ballooning of corruption in the Congress party and in Indian politics, here was a top level first-hand experience that corruption in the normal and legal sense, was not considered an offence at all by the highest level of political and executive authority in the state. To prosecute my predecessor might have opened a Pandora's box, which did open up forty years later. For those forty years this deep and widespread cancer was allowed to grow, to spread into the vicious shortages, black markets, *hawala*, and criminal politics. And all in the specious name of state socialism and development. That it started in Nehru's days was beyond doubt, only it did not surface beyond the Krishna Menon jeep scandal and the Mundhra affair, neither arousing much indignation from Prime Minister Nehru, who threatened to hang black marketeers from lamp posts. The press was not so alive; the public was still adoring its new 'nationalist' leaders, and was still credulous. I was told then that when corruption was drawn to Nehru's attention, he is alleged to have replied, 'Find me honest men!' Surely that itself was a function of India's first Prime Minister, the heir of Gandhi, and the darling of the masses who had full faith in him, leading the people to good government and out of poverty to the 'new temples' of development. That was perhaps the most alarming of the bells of Nostradamus; my first realisation that power was going into the hands of 'rascals, rogues, freebooters'. We had no idea in 1951 of just how far the cancer would grow. It was in that year when we, the people of India, gave ourselves the great white hope of the future, the Constitution, our charter of public virtue in the polity.

Three years later, and seven years after Independence, I was trekking in the remote Kumaon hills with a Swiss friend. Suddenly an old bespectacled man came round a bend, his hand held by his granddaughter. He stopped in his tracks on seeing a white man, and peering at us through thick glasses, in a state of excitement he addressed my Swiss friend: 'You knew how to rule. You administered justice. You were not corrupt.' I explained to him that he was mistaking him for the *angrez* or British whom he had heard of in India, and that this Swiss came from a different country. He gave me an unforgettable, touching reply: '*Koi bat nahi. Wohi murti hain.*' This old man in the remote hills may not have known the details of the history of the British Indian empire, of economic exploitation, of Jallianwala Bagh; but he conveyed the common man's verdict on pre- and post-1947 rulers.

I had a wonderful time in my few years in the early IAS. No lack of challenges, no personal complaints. In fact, I received the Prime Minister's and the same Chief Minister's commendation through my Chief Secretary, 'On the excellent organisation of food distribution and relief measures in Darbhanga district (on the verge of famine then) publicly commended by the Prime Minister at Patna.' I received 'The commendation of government for getting the King's canal in Madhubani reexcavated by creating a spirit of self-help and enthusiasm amongst the local people, who under your guidance and leadership voluntarily surrendered their lands, and did all the manual labour for the excavation of the canal and completed the project in forty-eight days only, without any financial or technical assistance from government or any other agency.' (Earlier the Public Works Department Minister wished to censure me for this same work. It seemed to take away the 'making' from *theka* or contract from him and his department). I also received the President's silver medal, 'In recognition of your outstanding zeal and the quality of services rendered by you during the 1951 Census of India.' Enough for any IAS Officer in his first five years. My DM and IAS colleague, Ujjal Ghosh hoped this would 'inspire me to keep up the quality of good work in future.'

This was my chosen profession from boyhood. I really thought there was no better. And yet, here I was disturbed by the shape of things to come, contemplating resignation from India's most prestigious service. If and when the muck surfaced, I felt I could not live with it. This was not the reason why I joined the civil service, to survive or wallow in the muck. I did not join for salary. But before I put in my resignation, I thought I should share my thoughts confidentially with four senior ICS officers of the state and get their advice. To my surprise, none of them gave me a single reason why I should stay on. I wondered why they stayed on. That helped me come to the sad and hard decision to resign. I have never regretted it. I made up my mind then, that I would serve the government in any honorary role, which I have done on committees, a Task Force, even the Board of a public corporation, never on the pay roll. Twenty years later, when D.P. Dhar, Central

Minister for Planning asked me to join the Planning Commission as Industrial Adviser, I turned it down. Mr. Deve Gowda (the former Prime Minister) asked the same Planning Commission, 'What went wrong?' He should have put that question to the people of India for better answers.

Market and Polity: Confounded Leadership

Why do I use the word confounded rather than confused? Because my dictionary tells me that confusion implies perplexity, disorder; and confounded adds the pejorative shamefully and cursedly to perplexity and disorder. The latter seems more appropriate to me, after seeing forty years of the unlearning, perverse politics of the polity in India, at the cost of competitive markets and the public interest. The confounding of polity and market has been a shame and a curse on an intelligent, enterprising people, who have performed far better abroad where markets are more open and competitive. In India there is a jinx on Indians between polity and market.

Market has, as always, been a biased word, recalling rapacious traders and money-lenders from the days pre- and post-Shakespeare's Shylock. It has no idealists, beyond a few Thatcherites and the International Monetary Fund (IMF). Various forms of polity have been idealised, atleast at the start. Those ideals varied from the *dharmashastras* of India, to the personalised monarchy of the Bourbons, to the dictatorship of the proletariate of the Bolsheviks. (Both, monarchy and dictatorship, were found out in 1789 and in 1989, exactly two centuries apart.) Democracy has been idealised since Pericles' days in Athens (though it was dependent on slavery then), to the British unwritten and American and Indian written Constitutions. Nehru's secular, socialist, planned democracy was another idealisation, now gone sour like the others. The realities proved to be very different in each case.

Consider a cup of coffee we all drink, as a representative symbol of the market, a vast invisible organisation to produce, process, brand, transport, buy and sell universally. No state has been able to produce metaphorical cups of coffee so universally accepted, because it has never been able to efficiently match that long organised chain, from Brazilian or Nilgiri plantations to that hot aromatic cup served so easily on your breakfast table. The USSR tried it for seventy years, and look what happened to that polity usurping the market. The Burmese polity is in backwaters, because it cut itself off from the world market after 1962. India was in a similar but worse plight in 1991, after forty years of a sheltered market. With no competition, an economy increasingly manipulated and plundered by the so-called trustees of the polity, politicians and bureaucrats, the treasuries were bankrupt, the nation's books were bulging with debts and India was on the verge of default in mounting debt payments caused by an improvident polity incapable of good financial management.

In his John Gaus lecture of 1995, Charles E. Lindblorn has said, 'No world state exists to match the world market.'

However imperfect, the market provides the world with a better coordinated supply of a thousand goods and services, than the United Nations' (UN) services to peace, international order, security, or health and cultural services; or the shortage, corruption-ridden 'markets' of controlled states. No government or international organisation can match the systematic coordination of millions of people, which goes to make the market; that silent, amazing, unsung institution. Ask the Russians outside the privileged 'nomenclature' what they thought of the market, pre-1989, run by ideological commissars. If there are any discontented Russians post-1989, it is because the USSR denied them market institution-building for seventy years, when most of the world was doing so. China is now trying to make a compromise since 1979, after its long march to Mao's hell, the tyrannical state promising ideological heaven. The ideological states, Hitler's, Stalin's, Tito's, Mao's or even Nehru's softer socialist state were morality plays and masquerading power systems.

In different roles, the market and the polity have complementary roles, especially in democratic polities. Both are imperfect human institutions, only the market is more easily correctable in a functioning democracy than the state of most polities in the real world. The powerful state is far more difficult to correct, with its organised power systems. What does the real world show? At one extreme, there is Ethiopia and Afghanistan, where no proper markets can flourish, as the state itself has generated disorder, and cannot provide the basic peace and security for those unsung millions to operate a peaceful, efficient market.

India has Bihar, Uttar Pradesh and the North-East. At the other extreme, are the stable democratic states, Germany, France, Britain, USA, Canada, Japan, Malaysia, Singapore, etc., where markets have flourished for the prosperity of its citizens, and where state and market make periodic adjustments, according to the democratic public opinion changes of these societies. There too, stable and strong institutions have been built up to regulate markets, to act as intermediaries between state and market, and to run markets efficiently.

India has been confused for most of the years since 1947. First, the dominant Congress party — the obvious successor to the British — did not do its real homework in the making of a modern polity and a modern economy in Asian conditions beyond passing superficial resolutions at its annual meetings between 1931 and 1947. Second, when the Indian ministries came to power in the states — 1936 to 1939 — only Gandhi saw the true rapacious nature of Indian politicians and Indian society, and so, in 1947 after Independence, he recommended the dissolution of the Congress party for Indian society to choose its new rulers. But the Congress was too eager to seize power, and Nehru, its leader, too infatuated with borrowed ideological dreams of the USSR and the Fabian society, which had no place for the market made by millions. He preferred a doctrinaire Planning Commission and the commanding heights of the state, which then brought us to the brink of bankruptcy in 1991 after forty years of economic and human development failures, with a trebling of population to command those failures. For forty years politico-bureaucratic planning was good; the market was bad, despite changes in global ideas and experience. Ideology became a mindless but profitable dogma for politicians and bureaucracy.

Even democratic polities have to be based on four major determining factors. They are : (a) ideologies rooted in the society's normative beliefs, not imported like a can of beans; (b) institutional, constitutional, legal, administrative, market, and social, which too are those which a society inherits and can operate successfully; (c) civil society which ensures a basis of social transactions in peace and amity; and (d) the crucial culture or cultural values by which societies conduct themselves. In 1947, India had no intrinsic ideology beyond Gandhiji's vague *Ram Raj*. So Nehru imported state socialism from his model, the USSR. Neither had a place for the market. India had a very high standard of administrative institutions, inherited from the British, in which Indians had been inducted, and were increasingly operating over half a century. These included a nationwide infrastructure, and a national market, with banks and stock exchanges. These were far more advanced than those of any other Asian or African colony. They have since run down, as East Asia surpassed India after 1965. Leaders or intellectuals did not bother much about civil society, taken for granted by the ideological presumptions of a *sirkari* culture, or cultural values relevant for economic and social development in the modern world. The apparatus of a modern government-controlled economy went with traditional corruption.

So engrossed was Nehru's generation in the passion for a Pink Ideology of the state, and they ignored the needs of a real civil society and Indian cultural factors so much, that they assumed India's inherited institutions would continue to function in the decades ahead with a kind of automatic efficiency, with the market in the background, controlled and run by the omniscient state. The first generation dreamers, obsessed with the *mantra* of an ideology of state planning to cure all security, economic, and social problems, lost control of the institutions of government itself in a steady deterioration post-1969. It had no faith in a sound civil society, or in the spirit of democracy, beyond the mechanics and the machinations of elections and legislatures. It had no faith in the market, even after millennia of Indian enterprise in India and the Indian ocean area, even after the Tatas, the Birlas, the Godrejs, the Sarabhais, the Bajajs, the Pochhanawalas and many others had led the way. The Nehruvian 'culture of *sirkar*', modern only in its specious externals, bred under the surface an atavistic culture of a new breed of plundering, feudal politicians, a culture of caste and corruption, a criminalisation of politics which undermined the frail foundation of a traditional civil society. Freedom was replaced by fiat; the market by the license and permit. Feudal authoritarianism got the better of Indian polity and Indian society, till the year of bankruptcy and reckoning in 1991, the year of a one-eyed awakening. It has since been only half an awakening, and half a reversion to the wrong *swadeshi* atavism.

Since being forced into liberalisation and globalisation by past failures and the compulsions of huge debt repayments in 1991 — not out of conviction — there have been two major failures. First, the process of liberalisation was expressed in meaningless technocratic, IMF jargon as 'structural readjustment'. Politicians and the state, especially the governing Congress party, failed to coin political messages to the people in the language of the people :

— that India would cease to be an insignificant 0.5 per cent economy in world trade;

— that the energies and initiatives of the people would be released for India to be a global player in the fields of her potentials, such as space satellites, textiles, gems and jewellery, machinery, agricultural products, software, tourism, etc.;

— that economic growth rate over 7 per cent p.a. was the only hope of lifting poverty, ill-health and illiteracy after forty years of low growth;

— that India would be no less confident in inviting large foreign investments as China and East Asia in critical sectors as infrastructure, particularly energy and transport, oil exploration and telecommunications;

— that India would make a purposeful thrust into the twenty-first century with a strong market democracy, with the state playing a more limited, but effective role.

But such a coherent message did not come from Mr. Narasimha Rao and Dr. Manmohan Singh to the people of India, and to the world. Their message was a negative assurance : 'Liberalisation is irreversible.' What it promised was not explained. That was a strategic failure of communications in a democracy, and in a globalising market — a huge political mistake too, which cost the Rao government defeat in the 1996 elections, apart from corruption.

The second failure was in the hangover of vested interest of the pre-1991 past, both in politics and in business. So, to defend their past, politicians still swore by the dated and failed 'Nehruvian model', bureaucrats were most reluctant to let go of power, and both were reluctant to give up the patronage which enlarged private fortunes like those of Sukh Ram and the *hawala* hordes and of corrupt businessmen, brought up in a protected market skilled in buying licenses, permits, and manipulating a control regime. Businesses began to make protective pleas for 'level playing fields', without specifying what that meant. Neo-swadeshists were back in the game, without Gandhi's logical clarity. They were emotional, nonfactual, confused, adhoc and trivial.

So there has been a schizophrenia, between atavistic tendencies which failed India between 1947 and 1991, and the global compulsion of technologies, trade and markets. Weak minds have nonfactually attributed the recent corruption revelations to liberalisation; when its sources went back to pre-1991 decades, especially the *hawala* tradition, Bofors, the Animal Husbandry scam and the bleeding of the banks. Weak men in power could reduce tariffs and taxes, but cowered before the hard leadership challenges of reducing deficits and overheads, disinvesting significantly in the public sector, and investing in social development, living up to the 'Open Skies' policy, opening up state monopoly in insurance, removing the Urban Land Ceiling Act, liberalising a too protective Industrial Disputes Act which pampered a secure, privileged 8 per cent of the total work force in government and the organised sector. Government itself is afraid of competition and wishes to play the combined role of regulator and player, a role that the men and women of straw and cardboard are unable to carry out efficiently and honestly.

So, in India, there has been no alternative political thinking since 1991, no political debate as to how to get out of the 0.5 per cent economy rut, how to be a global economic power comparable with China and East Asia.

The critical choice of the polity and the society is between treating the state as the 'Holy Cow', with its unproductive, wasteful manpower and expenditure growth for the benefit of no more than about 10 to 20 million in the state apparatus; or the productive, fifth largest world market of India for the benefit of hundreds of millions. That is the choice of Indian democracy, and true Indian democrats. In 1950, 360 million Indians produced goods and services worth US $ 50 billion. In 1995, 925 million Indians produced five times those goods and services worth US $ 2,550 billion. They could have produced far more, with less inflation, as East Asians have done, without the shackling license-permit-inspector raj. Till 1980, Gross Domestic Product (GDP) grew at only 3.5 per cent p.a., per capita income at only 1.5 per cent p.a., exports at about 6 per cent p.a. In the year of reckoning, 1991, GDP shrank to 0.9 per cent and the treasuries were empty. By 1995, with the growing recognition of the importance of the market, GDP rose to 6 per cent p.a. and industrial growth rose to 8 per cent p.a. Nearly 400 million people now constitute that market and its votes. Let politicians and bureaucrats see that irreversible writing on the wall of Indian market democracy.

The market, national and international, is a gigantic voluntary mechanism of choice, rejection, and adjustment; another kind of democracy in which people of all strata vote with their purchasing power and the freedom to choose. To moderate its imperfections, to help bring economic justice, to regulate the markets negotiations effectively, the polity and state need to play : (a) an effective regulatory role, not that of a failed monopolist, and an unproductive drainer of wealth; (b) a vigorous promoter role of the infrastructure's market; (c) an activist role in human development in education and health to enable more millions to enter the market as employers and employees, and as consumers with a higher quality of life; and (d) play its forgotten role as an enforcer of law and order for people and market to grow in peace. Polity and society also need to encourage the growth of a host of intermediate organisations between state and market for the growth of a civil and prosperous society. This involves a huge qualitative change of government, market, and society. The later chapters will explain why. They lie in the answers to Mr. Deve Gowda's question, 'What went wrong?'

The Half Per Cent Economy and The Spastic State

A spastic is an intelligent mind in an unwilling body.

— UNICEF

In 1950, after over a century of colonial rule, India's share of world trade was 2 per cent. After fifty years of Independence, of economic planning, after crores of investments, a panoply of Export Promotion Councils, India's share had shrunk to only 0.5 per cent. After the same fifty years and thousands of crores of investments, India's share of one of the fastest and longest growing trades, international tourism is only 0.4 per cent. With India's matchless attraction of natural phenomena, historic architecture, and cultures; foreign arrivals grew by only 1.7 per cent p.a. when the world figure was 4.6 per cent p.a., and in East Asia it was up to 14 per cent p.a. While India received only 1.5 million tourists recently, China received

19 million. India is among the 10 largest industrial countries, but it ranks 39 in the overall index of world competitiveness, as a result of its inefficiencies, profligate and wasteful government expenditures, and low productivity. Its scientific and technological numbers are supposed to be the third highest in the world, but its expenditure on Research and Development is one of the lowest among ranking countries at only 0.6 per cent, when advanced countries invest 2 per cent to 6 per cent. Prior to liberalisation, India's foreign exchange reserves were only 0.7 per cent of the world's total. That is not the end of poor performance.

In the Human Development Index, (HDI), India has fallen from a low 82 among world countries in 1970, to 134 in 1992, the most shameful reflection on the planned state. In HDI values, only countries like Nigeria and Bangladesh are below it. After forty years of development planning, India has the largest number of poor and illiterate in the world. Its child mortality rate was the highest in the world, barring Kenya and Niger.

By its own standards, i.e. those of the Prospective Planning Division of the Planning Commission, India has lagged about fifteen years or more. It is a timeless economy in a jet age. The constitutional target of free primary education in ten years has not been achieved in forty years, and nearly half the population is still illiterate; more so our women. Dr. F. Mehta had shown earlier in 1990 that :

— in foodgrains production we were about twelve years behind the targets of 1975-76;

— in finished steel we were about twenty-five years behind earlier targets of 1975-76;

— in coal we were fifteen years behind the 1975-76 target, and the same in aluminium.

India's endemic delays and cost overruns in nearly all projects have been notorious in a closed, uncompetitive economy. With inflation, those mounting costs and delayed materialisation have bled the country of countless hundreds of crores. And there has been no public accountability for it. No heads have rolled. The system gives security to the inefficient. The Public Accounts Committee has been either belated, or has had no teeth. The passion has been for large expenditures; result-orientation is unknown.

India has been a country of the future, a high potential country since the Fifties. It has had so many advantages over others in Asia and Africa. Yet the 'miracle' happened in East Asia between 1965 and 1990, while India lagged behind. What were the positive and negative lessons of East Asia, lost on an insular, self-righteous India in this period? First, a lack of good governments with efficient bureaucracies, which were friendly to investments, foreign ideas, and global technologies. Second, the East Asian countries fostered competition, and were not afraid of it, as India has been congenitally. Third, they were not prisoners of any ideology; they were pragmatic, experimental and reformist. So while Japan has passed its 'miracle', China is in 'a mid-miracle mode', India is still waiting for its 'miracle'.

What indeed, went wrong? Why is India a 0.5 per cent economy in the world's trade? Why, after all the planning and investment, did it shrink to a quarter of what it was in colonial days? Why, with the same planning, has it shrunk to the bottom of the scale in the HDI? Obviously, the planning was bad, and the implementation worse, with nil public accountability in a democracy, for a start.

What has risen? Population, inflation, crime, corruption, and most of all, government expenditures. A spastic has been defined by UNICEF as 'an intelligent mind in an unwilling or disobedient body.' The intelligent mind is that of Indians in India and abroad; the unwilling or disobedient body is the Indian state. The intelligent spastic has to be freed from this unwilling body. The energies and initiatives of the nation have to be released.

Anyone desiring to rise out of poverty and prosper, be it an individual, a family, company or state, needs to do the following simple things. When they don't, they fail.

1. To save, which means expenditure must be less than income, and if there is need to borrow, then those borrowings have to be serviced from surplus income.
2. To invest surpluses and borrowings profitably, so as to raise one's assets progressively to generate more surpluses.
3. To do these they need to raise productivity, manage resources efficiently, and in the case of companies (all sectors) and the state, to promote technological innovation and be competitive, nationally and internationally.

The Indian state and its public sector has failed on all these counts. It has been profligate and wasteful with the tax payer's and the nation's limited resources. In 1980, it had a budget deficit of Rs. 2,477 Cr. above total receipts and revenue, and a capital of Rs. 19,579 Cr., or 12.65 per cent beyond its earnings. Its fiscal deficit that year was Rs. 8,023 Cr., or 41 per cent above its earnings. In the budget of 1995-96, the budgetary deficit rose to Rs. 5,000 Cr., and its fiscal deficit to Rs. 57,634 Cr., or 3 per cent, and 34.5 per cent above its earnings, respectively. India's gargantuan fiscal deficits, even in the five years after liberalisation, has been 63 per cent (or Rs. 19,855 Cr.) in 1995-96 higher than the combined figure of the previous three years. The monster's appetite is uncontrollable, and mainly for the Establishment's own survival. That Establishment is an amoeba, the nation's parasite.

During this period, the people of India raised the total receipts of its Central government from Rs. 19,579 Cr. to Rs. 1,67,151 Cr., or an increase of 853 per cent in fifteen years. Yet this profligate, wasteful state could not live within an 853 per cent increase in its receipts. So the Indian state lurched into heavy borrowings, both internal and external. In 1980, India's external debt was US $ 1,407 million and its debt service ratio was 9.3 per cent. By 1993 it had jumped to US $ 8,942 million with a debt service ratio of 28.4 per cent. The major reason for the 1991 crisis was that India's external debt had doubled to Rs. 80,000 Cr. in the previous five years, when in the previous thirty-five years, it had risen to Rs. 40,000 Cr. Hence India was on the verge of payment defaults. This was a combination of financial profligacy and reckless financial mismanagement by all concerned, viz, Reserve Bank of India (RBI), Finance ministry and Parliament. The government's credit needs, now used for paying salaries and interest on past borrowings, account for half the nation's debt burden. Now that India's external debt has hit the US $ 100 billion mark, its lack of export capacity to repay is given below in comparison with other countries.

Ratio of Repayment Capabilities of Gross Debt

India	: 290	% of exports of goods and services.
Indonesia	: 219	% of exports of goods and services.
Malaysia	: 44	% of exports of goods and services.
Korea	: 48	% of exports of goods and services.
China	: 158	% of exports of goods and services.

In this critical area, the spastic's incapacity shows clearly in relation to other Asian countries. Developing countries like China and Mexico were attracting ten to fifteen times more foreign direct investment. India's investment prospects were poor despite its large market potential, because of a controlled economy, bureaucratic dilatoriness, and a weak infrastructure, in short, bad government. It was a spastic state, which did not invite investors by its performance. Even Dr. I.G. Patel, once at the helm of economic affairs, admitted the government had been 'reckless', 'the credibility of successive Indian governments is going down,' and 'unnecessary controls are seen as keeping that dynamism (of the nation) in check.' (*The Economic Times* 8.1.91).

The recklessness of the spastic is also shown in the seven times increase in food and fertiliser subsidies, from Rs. 1,110 Cr. to Rs. 7,347 Cr. in the Eighties; most of which went to the non-poor and richer farmers.

As a consequence, the people of India, especially its 350 million poorest, have had to suffer the highest inflation rates in Asia (with Indonesia). Past inflationary history has shown inflation as the worst killer; 'inflation as a government addiction makes society barbaric, and civilised society impossible.' Nothing mortgages the future of a society as inflation.

Yet we have not seen the end of government's past lack of responsible prudence and uncontrollable profligacy. Our children will be burdened with the iron weight of repayments of multiple proportions, indications of which are given below:

Repayment Schedule for Market loans (Rs. Crores)

Fiscal Years	Central Government	State Government
1995-96 to 1998-99	22,072	2,314
1999-2000 to 2003-04	55,499	9,101
2004-05 to 2011-12	58,330	22,656

These figures show how damagingly past governments of all parties have mortgaged India's future for the next twenty years. (Source : *The Economic Times* 2.10.95) Since 1981, India's total debt has multiplied ten times from Rs. 59,797 Cr. to Rs. 6,05,869 Cr. by March, 1996. If the debts of public sector and local bodies are added, it amounts to Rs. 9,10,970 Cr., or fifteen times, a drunken debtor. India's high indebtedness and high inflation has contributed to the depreciation and the devaluation of the rupee to the US dollar which now costs Rs. 36 to Rs. 37, when till only two years ago it was Rs. 31.37 and in the early Eighties it was Rs. 16. Any Indian family with this record, without the power to mint money, and to borrow so heavily, would have gone to the wall. Our politicians are driving the Indian people to the wall, whilst they enrich themselves. So now there is not enough money to pay for India's defence security, for infrastructure, for health, education and poverty alleviation, all the things that past planning was intended to provide.

Governments committed to national planning had, even before 1980-81, wildly increased non-plan expenditures. In 1980-81 it was Rs. 13,062 Cr., in 1994-95 it was Rs. 1,05,117 Cr. or eight times more, and this was largely because irresponsible borrowing had raised interest charges from Rs. 2,604 Cr. to Rs. 46,000 Cr., or over seventeen times; partly because irresponsible subsidies (more to the non-poor than the poor) had been raised from Rs. 2,028 Cr. (1980-81) to Rs. 9,463 Cr. (1994-95), and had further risen to Rs. 12,400 Cr. till 1993-94. So in this period expenditure on agriculture, rural development and irrigation rose from Rs. 2,231 Cr. (1985-86) to only Rs. 8,934 Cr. (1994-95), or only four times. Social services expenditures rose from Rs. 1,693 Cr. (1985-86) to Rs. 7,381 Cr. (1994-95), also only four times. These were supposed to be the favoured electorate. Yet the people of India had raised their taxes from Rs. 13,149 Cr.

(1980-81) to Rs. 87,136 Cr. (1994-95), or six times more to cope with the burdens imposed by politicians.

What have the politicians done with the six times higher taxes, and the fifteen times higher borrowings?

1. They have imposed one of the two highest rates of inflation in India on 950 million people, especially on the 350 million, the poorest and 550 million, the middle class. Even after 1990-91, the year of financial disaster, the economy grew at an average rate of only 4 per cent p.a., but they pumped in additional money at 18 per cent p.a., by minting and borrowing to help a rapacious government survive, and not for the growth of the economy and the people.

2. Whilst the people of India have paid six times more taxes in the last fifteen years, politicians and bureaucrats have increased non-Plan expenditures for their own salaries, perks and enlargement of the government machinery after liberalisation and decontrol eight times, their interest charges on borrowings seventeen times, depriving India's children of health and education for the next twenty years. It does not matter to them that the rate of growth of their expenditures is about twice the rate of growth of the Indian economy, which involves serious risks to India's security, insecurity for millions of unemployed, hunger, and delayed hopes for 350 million below the poverty line; all condemned to their plight after the past fifty years, and for indefinite years to come.

These are irresponsible, avaricious, self-aggrandising governments, Centre and states, who presume to rule but cannot control their own appetites and personal empire-building. Even after liberalisation and decontrol, there are huge redundancies in Udyog Bhavan, Director General for Trade and Development, Krishi Bhavan; not to speak of the states where salaries are drawn for bloated non-functioning staffs on the pay-roll. Even after the dismantling of foreign trade controls, there has been the mockery of the office of the Chief Controller of Imports and Exports changing its name to Directorate General of Foreign Trade, with no reduction of staff and reduced functions. And what do the lakhs of redundant staff do? Clerks and peons comprise 97 per cent of government staffs, a long low-productive tail, consuming huge revenues, and delaying efficient growth, the unproductive weedy plants of politicians. They do three things for three quarters of their time.

First, for those who know that rotten machinery, they are low on productivity and high on red-tape and costly delays. After decades of the catchwords 'streamlining' and 'rationalisation' — endlessly promised by the governments to cure the problem — even after partial decontrol and liberalisation things haven't changed much.

— There are 385 rules to be followed under excise duty regulation.

— For industrial licensing 69 questions are asked and 82 more have to be answered if permission is required.

— For appointment of a Managing Director the Company Law Board asks 55 questions.

— An entrepreneur has to obtain clearances from 18 agencies under the Industries Development & Regulation Act, and has to face 61 inspectors. After he starts, he has to live with a rapacious inspector-raj of at least 6 inspectors for various purposes for the life of the enterprise.

— There is a plethora of No Objection Certificates (not necessary in law) invented by this *babugiri* to exact money, most objectionably, for hundreds of petty purposes. Our politicians of all parties repeatedly ask for unlimited foreign investments — taking Indian ones for granted — and yet they have a built-in interest in perpetuating the most notorious delaying-action bureaucracy in the world. Time has no price for them. They are indifferent.

Second, the purpose of all these low productivity, high cost barriers is to make every opportunity to loot and plunder the public, or investors as well as the government itself. Witness the classic loot of the Bihar treasury of Rs. 950 Cr. by the Animal Husbandry Department alone, a massive loot operation going on undetected for over a decade, involving politicians of many parties and successions of officials. Where was the state's Vigilance Commission? Or the vigilant press?

Loot and plunder is now the in-built counter-system, of which more is discussed in a later chapter on '*Sauda* alias Corruption.'

The third occupation of the government's gargantuan *babugiri* of millions is just plain departmental gossip over cups of tea. It is perhaps the largest gossip club in the world indulging in talk on postings, transfers, promotions, inter-personal relations of the bureaucracy and the power games within.

The nation's cake may not grow, but theirs must. Between 1973-74 and 1985-86, *The Economic Times* dated 23.11.90, reported per capita income of the Indians had gone up by 207 per cent, but the income of employees of public sector companies went up by 365 per cent, yet their productivity is the lowest. Some years ago, the Energy Minister, Vasant Sathe, revealed that in the public steel sector more than 1.5 lakh people produced 1 million tons of steel. The same was produced in developed countries by only 14,000 people. In coal, 7 lakh people produced what only 30,000 produced in Australia. The 'commanding heights' of the economy have become the demanding heights. Now the United Front Government Railway Minister declares the railways a 'welfare' institution, proposing to add 30,000 to its numbers, when a World Bank report found 4,00,000 of 1.7 million surplus. If the railways are not profitable, from where will the resources for their growth and modernisation come? The minister is only interested in his tenure, the future of the Indian Railways can go to the devil. It is the interest of these secure, privileged people that our 'pro-people' Left parties champion against policies of liberalisation for millions of Indians, amounting to 900 million middle class and those below the poverty line. Only 10 to 15 million in the government and public sector — excluding the Armed Forces — are the parasites who are pampered and who feed on the remaining 900 and more millions.

The plunder of the counter-system cannot even sustain itself now. Dr. Bimal Jalan, a long-time economic pandit in the Finance ministry, now believes the following in the wiser autumn of his long economic experience in government.

— There has to be expenditure control for long term sustainability of the fiscal deficit.

— Nearly a third of the interest liabilities are due to past investments in the public sector out of borrowings.

— India's debt profile is much worse than what was anticipated five years ago.

— Any feasible increase in taxes cannot take care of the debt problem.

— Public sector units cannot be made autonomous, and the only feasible way of reducing public debt and interest liabilities is to disinvest. It is no longer a question of ideology, but a matter of practical necessity.

— 'Government controls per se are not pro-poor.'

— Most importantly, 'Much of our strategic thinking reflects the colonial experience'; and 'the trade isolation of the past did not increase India's autonomy or strengthen the authority of the state. The fears of political dependence due to trade and investment are irrelevant in today's interdependent world for expanding economies.' (*The Times of India*, 10.9.96. Interview by Tapan Das Gupta).

This last is a clear message for the Left ideologies and the 'neo-swadeshist' from a man living within the system for the past decades, now emerging from that cocoon after a spell as India's Executive Director at the World Bank, Washington. It is amazing how such past Pandits of North Block change their views after leaving North Block. Those Blocks and Bhavans and our legislatures still reflect that legacy of the colonial experience. Most Indian politicians behave as if they were freebooters of India's eighteenth century, and have no notion of economic and technological competition in our times. They are two centuries behind. When Laloo Prasad Yadav described himself as the 'King of Bihar', he only indiscreetly expressed the feudal reflections of other politicians besides himself.

Freebooting for political populism is a common phenomenon from Centre to states. Men and women of cardboard have demonstrated this in cheap rice and prohibition in the South when they magnify themselves in cardboard cutouts, and drain the exchequer. Cheap rice and cheap power do not produce more rice and more power for more millions. A shocking document has been produced by the Andhra Pradesh government. The facts revealed by this document are given below.

— As a result of prohibition, there has been a fall of Rs. 1,000 Cr. in excise revenue. This seriously contracts social development expenditure for the poor, or compels more debts.

— Expenditure on establishment and pensions alone accounts for 85 per cent of the state's tax and non-tax resources. The corresponding figure for Government of India is 30 per cent, including the defence forces. About 40 per cent of the staff in the Irrigation department is surplus. A glaring example of the politicians of the spastic state using the government as 'a public dowry', in the words of the President Dr. Shankar Dayal Sharma himself.

— The largest drain on the Andhra Pradesh state is the losses of Public Sector Units (PSUs). With capital and loans of Rs. 2,600 Cr. in Andhra Pradesh State Electricity Board, the more power it produces the more it loses, because of the power supplied at below the cost price to farmers and to low tariff users. The government has converted the bulk of its loans to equity, and has then written it off. Cheap power is the surest way to no power and bankruptcy.

— Andhra Pradesh's PSUs give the state and the people a dividend of a mere Rs. 5.79 lakhs on an investment of Rs. 1,942 Cr., or 0.3 per cent for which, in its financial genius, it borrows at 14 per cent.

— Cheap rice in Andhra Pradesh is supposed to be for the 22 million below the poverty line. The actual figure is 11.2 million, the surplus of 11 million being bogus. All populist policies have been bogus in the states and in the Centre.

This is no government. It is the rake's dance of cinematic heroes in what should be a responsible government. Multiply all this twenty-eight times pro rata, and you have some idea of the financial lunacy of the Spastic States of India, which are considered to be trustees of the nation's resources.

This Spastic State of India cannot even utilise aid money efficiently. In 1980-81, there was Rs. 6,882 Cr. unutilised in the aid pipeline, constituting 25 per cent of total foreign aid. In 1989-90 it had multiplied seven times to Rs. 48,107 Cr., or 57.3 per cent. India has had to pay the World Bank, in that decade, US $ 260 million as commitment charges. The main reasons given for slow utilisation are delays in land acquisition, poor availability of counterpart funds, and a plethora of mandatory clearances, all within the incompetence of governments. Perhaps, in a proper reckoning, it is possible that the costs of this inefficient aid management is higher than its benefits.

Are these not massive, inexcusable economic offences by governments themselves?

Now, in 1996, at long last, the RBI is sufficiently alarmed to assert some independent firm views, after decades of deference to Finance ministry. It has cautioned against any deterioration of the liabilities position of the government which seriously undermines the very credibility of its fiscal policy. It has called for a ceiling in law on a runaway public debt. It is a pathetic irony that a government which asks all Indians, Non-Resident Indians (NRI) and foreigners to invest in India, cannot save itself, and has brought down the national saving's rate from a high of 24 per cent to below 20 per cent. With large deficits politicians, especially of the Left and the so-called socialists, fail to realise they make a nonsense of development planning, by which they swear, and defeat higher social development expenditures in health and education, and poverty alleviation, which they claim is the foundation of their dated, abused ideology. The urge to plunder overcomes the specious declaration to develop. The RBI recommends abandoning budget deficits, and concentrating on the total fiscal deficits, which is more realistic. And when these are expressed as small percentages of GDP, they are a statistical ruse to show a small figure. India's debts are not paid from a statistical concept like GDP. They can only be paid from real resources mobilised by way of taxes and savings, export earnings, and a favourable trade balance. The RBI also stresses more disciplined liquidity management and assistance to Centre and states by specific Ways and Means Advances, and not treated as perpetual financing devices, as if national resources were limitless, even for profligates.

In short, the government's economic and fiscal policies should be that of a responsible, prudent householder, not that of a self-aggrandising gambler. For those who act like undisciplined gamblers, and then fall back on traditional Indian values, the first value that all Indian governments should cultivate is that of *dharmic grihasts*. Indian democracy must ensure it for its own survival. When will we see the *dharmic grihast* in a political manifesto?

Infrastructure Sinews and Men of Straw

Greed and evil are king and minister, falsehood their officer; lust the counsellor who is called for advice. All three hold conclave to chalk out plans. The subjects, bereft of understanding, are carcasses full of straw.

— Adi Granth
Asa-ki-Var, M.I. pp 468-69.

In the last five to ten years, the problems of India's infrastructure has boggled the minds of many from the World Bank to foreign and local investors, infrastructure professionals, the press, all except the politicians and technocrats so involved in their own games. Only Maharashtra is now keen on privately run and managed super highways. Changing Railway Ministers make places like Malda and Hajipur new, wasteful, and low priority employment centres in their political constituencies. There are hardly any macro conceptualisers and policy framers, even in the Central Cabinet. The Indian penchant for adhocery, delays, and imprudent expenditures prevail. There is no national energy policy nor a surface transport policy. Nor a re-examination of the major/medium irrigation policies which were condemned by no less a person than the former Prime Minister Rajiv Gandhi in 1986. The post-JRD Tata phase of Indian aviation has steadily gone down the bureaucratic, monopolistic road, though a few struggling private airlines have made a difference, despite the lack of 'open skies' and level playing fields. Irrigation systems and nationalised banks have been national liabilities, their future uncertain.

In national seminars a fundamental question has been posed: is the basic problem a lack of sound comprehensive policies, or a bad decision-making process? It is both these and much more. In energy, besides the lack of national policies, there is weak implementation, a political interest in unviable underpricing, leakage and theft of power, no national grid, nor an overall regulatory authority for power, and bad decision-making. In Telecom the absence of a regulatory authority has led to adhoc, arbitrary, corrupt decision-making, throwing up a major scandal around the Central Cabinet Minister, Sukh Ram, dithering and ambiguity in both policy and decisions. India's ports have long been the neglected children of Indian infrastructure, and the most inefficient in Asia; weak technological and labour managements, and divided responsibilities between the states for minor ports, and the Centre for larger ports. There are more divisions in responsibilities as far as roads are concerned, from district roads to national highways. It was very surprising to read the view of a National Transport Policy Committee in 1979, that there were no new technologies in transport; revealing the backwater minds of the New Delhi bureaucracy. To the extent that Urban Development — perhaps the first challenge of the twenty-first century — is mainly an infrastructure problem, it is not on the political agenda; and the Ministry for Urban Development seems primarily engaged in allotting scarce accommodation to demanding V.I.Ps in office, and then finding it hard to eject them when they demit office. This too has been the subject of controversy and scandal.

All these suffer from a lack of resources, a lack of specialised continuity and political stability, the lack or shortcomings of national policies, widespread cost over-runs and inefficiency, and widespread corruption. That also presents the face of official India, a face that is not very inviting to foreign investors in infrastructure; more so after the experiences of Enron and Cogentrix. This is very disappointing to Indian investors, whose national savings rate could rise to 24 per cent, even though East Asia's is over 30 per cent. The United Front government's estimate of infrastructure requirements in the next five years is of the order of US $ 200 billion. It is a pipe dream, a fantasy wish; given the resources position, the lack of clear national policies and political will, and the built-in political interest in underpricing and subsidising infrastructure services, technological ineptitude of government power, water and transport systems, and as always, plain cheating and corruption, quite apart from lack of real will and fiscal incentives for private sector participation in both production and distribution of power and in other sectors. The total capital issues in infrastructure utilities in 1994-95 was only Rs. 767 Cr., with nothing in railways (save Rs. 480 Cr. in 1993-94) and in roadways since 1991-92. This is a clear indication of the lack of political will and resources. Yet even now, the present Railway Minister regards the Indian railways as an instrument of 'welfare', and not of viable profitability. If it is so, then from where will future growth and modernisation come? These mindless men of straw exist only for their own tenure. The devil take the country and its people.

Take power, against an Eighth Plan target of 40,000 MW additional capacity to maintain the same level of shortage (mark the endemic failure of state planning to meet higher demand), real additional capacity was a mere 18,000 MW. Plant load capacities in the public power sector, after four decades of state operation, cannot exceed 50 per cent, when private sector plants are over 95 per cent. In some states it is between 20 per cent and 40 per cent only. No power system anywhere in the world is sustainable with 50 per cent load factors, and 20 per cent to 35 per cent wastages and theft. Yet there is no political will, no bureaucratic or technical thrust to remedy these known failures over the past thirty years. Planning has become an on-going exercise in magnifying losses.

The root of the biggest single national disaster in infrastructure has been in the power sector, and no government has mobilised the political will and capacity to go to the heart of the problem, which is uneconomic tariffs, non-payment of dues right up the line, monopoly of the public sector in oil exploration with a constriction to Indian basins only, administered oil and natural gas prices leading to unsustainable distortions in subsidised pricing and imports, apart from increased pollution. In 1984-85, Indian oil fields produced 66 per cent of total crude oil needs; it is now producing 45 per cent (decline increasingly dependent on high sulpher oil imports). Almost 40 per cent to 50 per cent of the power of State Electricity Boards (SEBs) is not even metered. The overall sale of power to the Agricultural sector registered a steep fall from 77 per cent in 1960-61 to 51 per cent in 1993-94. That is the major area of loss and theft. The SEBs earn their meagre revenues by selling only about 40 per cent of the energy generated, and the balance 60 per cent is losses and agricultural consumption, free political lunches.

Due to widespread theft, waste and connivance, payments are not made for power consumed by users (especially rich farmers, the political base of Members of Parliament and Members of Legislative Assembly) to SEBs. The SEBs cannot pay the National Thermal Power Corporation (NTPC). Outstanding dues to NTPC on 30.09.95 were as high as Rs. 3,355 Cr., the highest being in the Northern states who were responsible for 80 per cent of these non-payments, including the centrally administered Delhi Electricity Supply Undertaking (DESU). The Centre's counter-guarantees to power projects could be of the order of Rs. 10,000 Cr. p.a., or a staggering Rs. 2,00,000 Cr. over twenty years. The cumulative outstandings of SEBs is over Rs. 45,000 Cr. Neither state nor Central governments can guarantee payments to any one, including new private investors who are now being invited to invest heavily in a business without payments, the very basis of any sensible market, which even the Marxists cannot deny. The game of the past called the Nehruvian Model — of which Nehru would have disapproved in its later manifestations, but which his party has followed — was that each lives off the other and no one is responsible for payments and viability. The nation pays the huge price. And this is supposed to be an economic model for growth!

Unless this root problem is cured by political will and public opinion, the whole economic and security problem of India will get bogged down in the morass of the power sector. The stakes are no less. Modern societies run on energy. The men of straw in the past thirty years have knowingly created this problem. Only real leadership can save the nation from this disastrous ransom to rich farmers, dishonest businessmen, and corrupt politicians and administrators. Orissa has set an example by abolishing the SEB.

One sees the same non-paying and non-sustainable irresponsibility in the public sector beyond power in irrigation, in the banks, in cities, and now in the State Trading Corporation (STC). Controller and Auditor General (CAG) found bad debts of Rs. 80 Cr. as 'receivables'. With this STC was able to show a profit of Rs. 35 Cr. in 1995-96, and a dividend to its owner, the government, of Rs. 9 Cr. But the same owner had been STC's bad debtor of Rs. 80 Cr. for over three years, and hence the valid CAG view. A bad debt is a bad debt whether in government or business. The books cannot be fudged so blatantly. This undeniable fact was being covered up, despite CAG's disclosing comments.

After that core problem, the entire future costing of the power sector needs a thorough review, and a fundamental change from state capitalism's past addiction to large expenditures, large *thekas,* huge leakages, subsidies and enormous kick-backs. The very need for large new capacities is in question, with inefficient low plant-load factors, the low tension lines and corrupt inefficient distribution systems.

One way to optimise existing capacities and transmission and distribution losses estimated at 23 per cent (6 per cent to 10 per cent only in developed countries), is to go over to three-phase distribution transformers and a switch-over from low tension to high tension distribution systems to avoid voltage drops, high line losses, and unauthorised connections. The Centre for Policy Research ('Ground Realities', *The Business Times,* 12.8.96) has shown that, a reduction of every 1 per cent of transmission and distribution losses in India is equivalent to an addition of about 1,200 MW of generation capacity to the present installed capacity of 72,000 MW. Andhra Pradesh Electricity Board has conducted extensive studies to establish that distribution losses can be brought down to the levels of advanced countries by changing over to the single-phase system, which offers the following advantages :

— distribution losses can be reduced by 75 per cent and more;

— system faults are reduced because of the length of low voltage lines;

— in the single-phase system only a few consumers are connected to the transformer, reducing the chances of unauthorised connections and theft.

On the basis of a plant load factor of 60 per cent, and the above savings amounting to Rs. 4 Cr. per MW, for a reduction of transmission and distribution losses to even 15 per cent from 23 per cent, 9,600 MW can be saved, (or half the installed capacity of the Eighth Plan), with a saving in cost of Rs. 38,400 Cr. Besides, savings in consumption also has enormous scope. The Pune-based energy analyst, Prayas has shown that efficient utilisation could save 25 per cent of the cost, and the power generating capacity of Maharashtra could come down to 55 per cent. We need to consider the concept of 'affordable power' in a new power policy. In the Prayas study, the least cost options for power seem to be the creation of new capacities through cost-based plants for base load, while pumped hydro could cater to peaking demands.

In no field of infrastructure, in no basic need have Indian governments been so far from realities as in the case of water. It requires no great brains to know that water is produced in the skies and from glacier mouths; it is held in forests, in soil, sub-soil regions, the rest is run-off into the seas, which in India is estimated to be 85 per cent of rainfall and snow-melt. Any geography student knows it. Our governments and their water specialists have assumed that water is produced by the application of huge amounts of money to dams, to canals, to pipelines, to tanks; in short, by engineering and plumbing. Nature's sources are ignored or taken for granted. A mindless technology flows from plans, projects, and expenditures. As, since Nehru, governments have sought to be the *sirkar*, the *Mai-Bap*, the god-like bestowers from Planning and the Treasury, like Bhagirath bringing down the Ganga. They have assumed a supply-driven approach. The supply-driven approach either assumes that water is an unlimited resource, or that it is not important to know its sources and its sustainability. Money, engineering, plumbing and the profitable *theka* with large expenditures are all that is needed. No result orientation or accountability is required. The people should be grateful receivers responding with the vote. Water projects, like other fruits of development, are free-meal tickets for the vote. The fact that such a supply-driven, free-meal ticket approach is economically unsustainable is now slowly dawning, as in the case of power.

Bhakra was Nehru's first 'temple' of development. He began the big dam business. His grandson, Rajiv realised and publicly admitted that after all the heavy investments in large-scale irrigation over decades, 85 per cent of the benefits of that gargantuan investment did not reach the farmers. 'Perhaps we can safely say almost no benefit has come to the people from these projects. For sixteen years we have poured money out. The people have got nothing back, no irrigation, no water, no increase in production, no help in their daily life.' In the years between the grandfather and the grandson, huge, costly, and irretrievable mistakes have been made, with Indian water technologists strapped to political chairs. How did that happen? What have been its enormous and tragic consequences?

Large dams built since, spending hundreds of thousands of crores have silted at four to sixteen times the earlier estimated rates, thus reducing their life spans. Though they were partly flood control measures, in 1953, floods affected upto 10 million people; in 1982, 54 million people, five times higher. Enormous human suffering has been caused by bad resettlement of dam oustees which has been totally unsatisfactory.

Let us look at the findings of Mr. B.B. Vohra, a distinguished member of the IAS, and a devoted student of India's natural resources of land, water and forests. (Source: 'Better Resources Management for Poverty Alleviation', *The Economic and Political Weekly*, 8.6.96). In water management, really mismanagement, B. B. Vohra reminds us of some of the main failures.

— Between 1950 and 1995 we have spent Rs. 50,000 Cr. on big, medium and small projects for surface storage capacity of 20 mh; in the Eighth Plan alone, Rs. 27,500 Cr. In the Seventh Plan, investment was Rs. 11,107 Cr. Major and medium projects 'resulted in a loss of 0.6 mh of even the potential of that which existed at the end of the Sixth Plan, and no gain in the Seventh Plan, earlier envisaged at 4.3 mh. The net loss of planned potential between 1985 and 1990 amounted to 4.9 mh, the replacement of which at current prices would be well in excess of Rs. 38,000 Cr., with no explanation offered so far by the Ministry of Water Resources as to how it took place!'

— The track record of small surface projects is worse. 'The net area served by such projects declined from 8.2 mh in 1961 to 6.8 mh in 1989, inspite of the fact that Rs. 6,000 Cr. were invested in them in the intervening 25 years!' Money that went down the drains and pockets.

— The additional area brought under irrigation between 1951 and 1990 by the major and medium sector was said to be 1.2 mh, raising the total figure to 25.1 mh. This means that as much as 13.9 mh (25.1 minus 11.2) of the total potential lay unused. During this period, in this sector, costs rose from Rs. 1,060 in the first plan to Rs. 42,600 per ha. in the Seventh Plan, and is now expected to be Rs. 70,000 mha.

In addition, there has been extensive damage by the erosion of top soil, estimated at 6,000 million tons p.a. — soil water-logging and salination, growing from 14 mh in 1981 to 27 mh in 1995. At an average cost of Rs. 4,000 per ha. curing water-logged and desalinated lands would cost Rs. 35,000 Cr. Where will this money come from? These leaders of straw, who want the votes of the farmer's, don't care.

The Congress and Janata parties, in particular, are supposed to be friends of farmers, their electoral base. In Mr. Deve Gowda we had a farmer's Prime Minister. What were they doing as political leaders, ministers and Chief Ministers when all these failures were being perpetrated by those in power, at such high cost to the farmers, the exchequer, and the nation over the last thirty years and more? In Maharashtra, 3 per cent of the sugar acreage has captured 75 per cent of the irrigated water as a result of the political power of the cooperative sugar barons, Maharashtra's politicians' war chest for over three decades. In the same 'advanced' state, only 75 per cent of the irrigation created is claimed to be utilised. Another example of plundering through cooperatives, on one side, and ignoring the majority of farmers in the state, on the other. The children of India will pay a heavy price for this irresponsibility concerning water in future. There can be no other need as basic as water for all life. Yet this criminal waste and plunder continues with no accountability and no correction, Mr. Deve Gowda.

A World Bank study (1992) showed the deterioration in India's irrigation system. In 1947, irrigation made a net contribution to government finances, and so after cost and payment systems, pre-Independence governments made it sustainable. By the 1980s irrigation subsidies accounted for 70 per cent of total agriculture subsidies, another example of the Indian politician's free-meal approach for votes at the cost of the poor farmer so far, and its unsustainable costs to the nation henceforth. Through sheer inefficiency and bad management, 142 major and 216 medium projects were left incomplete. After four decades of dams and irrigation, 70 per cent of Indian agriculture is still dependent on the rains! That is another mark of the men of straw in an area of critical national importance — more so, of national survival itself.

If India is a 0.5 per cent economy in world trade, it is partly due to the parlous state of our ports; between a non-enterprising bureaucracy, Asia's most unproductive working class at the docks, and the highest freight and port-handling charges in Asia. A Delhi-based political and bureaucratic system cannot see the economic and strategic advantage of ports with a long coastline; just as they have not seen the importance of Indian shipping and an Indian Navy, a pre-Vasco de Gama vision in land-locked minds.

The last World Bank report has shown how the men of straw in Delhi indulge in statistical pipe dreams which never materialise. They are, as usual, '*dikhane ke liye*'. They have given India an ambitious target of US $ 100 billion exports by the year 2001. No account has been taken of India's incapacity to handle this increase through inefficient ports and non-existing port capacities, apart from the nearly equal import figures! In the first three years of the Eighth Plan only 4.8 million tons of port capacity were added against planned 46.5 million tons. The National Planning Commission is a National Dreaming Commission. The last firm figures of 1993-94 were US $ 22.2 billion in exports, and US $ 23.8 billion in imports. How the dreamers are hoping to reach four times those figures with Asia's most inefficient infrastructure and port systems, puts the figure beyond realistic credibility. This has been a continuous trait of *sirkari* socialist planning for forty years. We aspire high, we perform low and there is never any accountability.

Low port-productivity levels are reflected in the present trend of one man-hour container at leading international ports, whereas in India it is a glaring 59 man-hours per container! Even by Asian standards Nhava-Sheva (India's latest supplement to Bombay), is a mere 10-12 containers per ship hour, against 69 in Singapore, 38 in Bangkok,

35 in Colombo and 22 in Penang. Most other Indian ports are even lower. Freight and port-handling charges in India are higher than that of her Asian competitors, China, Bangladesh, Thailand, Sri Lanka and Singapore. For this reason, foreign lines avoid direct calls and increasingly deploy feeders to tranship cargo to India through Colombo, Singapore, Dubai and Abu Dhabi.

Look at Bombay's coastline, and every day of the year there is a long line of waiting ships incurring high demurrage. The World Bank report estimates the cost of these inefficiencies at Rs. 875 Cr., or about 40 per cent of India's export earning in 1993-94. And here is a country crying out for foreign exchange earnings and foreign investments! No *swadeshi* politician or economist has raised his voice against this huge annual loss. Any serious privatisation of the ports will hit the hard rock of dock-labour vested interests, and the men of straw will, as in the case of banks, airlines, and public sector, cave in pusillanimously.

The hottest cake of the infrastructure recently has been telecommunications, with the eruption of the Minister Sukh Ram scandal. It was just waiting to be revealed after the goings on in the Department of Telecommunications (DOT) in the last two years. If any single technology involves a leap into the twenty-first century, it is telecommunications. The leap of crores into the minister's houses, and his minions is only a natural fallout of three main factors. These factors are : (a) the widespread 'systems failures' of government; (b) the archaic 1885 Indian Telegraph mind-sets of control systems, which invite corruption and dislike transparent competition; and (c) the incapacity of the governments to appreciate the technological implications of this very crucial and fast-changing industry linking many aspects of global communications, transcending national boundaries, computers, television, telecommunications via satellites, and all 'gone digital.' What is more, the fast growth has resulted in a sharp decline in prices. The price of Indian telephone sets have come down in two years from over Rs. 1,000 to Rs. 500, after Sam Pitroda's thrust into the private sector and the shattering of Indian Telephone Industry's dated monopoly. A classic example of the fall of PSUs from the 'commanding heights' brought about by technology, which is shattering ideology and old boundaries.

What is important in answer to 'What went wrong?,' is the lessons of this spectacular muck-up. Since Rajiv Gandhi and Sam Pitroda, his adviser, it was obvious for a decade that telecommunications would be the great new thrust area. In this, as in all other areas requiring large investments, the government is schizophrenic. The politicians say general welcoming words about the irreversibility of liberalisation, the advent of capital and technology, fast 'tracks', 'single window clearances', etc., and in this case, the high aspiration to connect all villages by telephone by 1997. The bureaucracy — inheriting colonial and post-colonial minds addicted to controls, with planning hardly going beyond some superficial physical and financial objectives doled out to impress the people and the media — fails to understand the economics, technologies, and management systems of a fast paced modern world. The bureaucracy is itself divided between the honest and the opportunist. The latter are the natural allies of politicians, the twin parasites.

In the second stage, Indian and foreign enterprise is initially impressed. India, the most controlled market outside USSR and Cuba is opening up. India, despite its poverty, is among the ten largest industrial economies in the world; its market promises to be among the five largest. It has a recognisable judicial system, and a vast pool of managerial, technological know-how. So they came. Tenders (the good old Indian *theka*) are invited. Indian business links up with global players. Then the government gets greedy for high license fees. The informal networks begin to operate, rules are changed to suit obliging parties, files are sat on; 'speed money' is the answer. Amidst all this, corruption seeps in and seeps out. The circus is paraded in the media over months in unfolding phases. The bureaucracy is paralysed in its leap into the twenty-first century, especially if there is a change in government or ministers. There is a sudden realisation that the Telecom Regulatory Authority should have come first, before the rule-twisting and the not-so-surreptitious money-grabbing.

In the third stage of private 'moolah', public *hu-ha*, and administrative paralysis, both foreign and Indian investors begin to have second thoughts. They lose their confidence. India ends up as the real loser, and the twenty-first century seems farther away! The corruption circus, and its political implications supercede India's vital telecom needs.

This three-part scenario, this 'failure of the system' is not unique in the DOT's case. Corruption or no corruption, it is typical. It manifested itself with variations, a generation ago over prospecting Indian oil resources. A good and really honourable minister, Ashok Mehta then recommended international standards in oil negotiations. An atavistic cabinet, afraid of an atavistic Parliament, was afraid to take that decision. Twenty precious years were lost in coming to the same decision, but in changed global conditions. Recently, one has seen the same scenario in the power sector, especially with Enron and Cogentrix, with similar delays and similar erosion of confidence. This stymied syndrome was also seen for years in arms purchases for the defence services after the Bofors scandal. We go from crisis to crisis, from high economic cost to higher economic cost; the scenario and the atavism persists. Only the details change. The world loses confidence in India. We lose confidence in the system.

Sukh Ram may have put vital decisions of government as well as Indian and foreign companies on the back-burner for an indefinite period. What is relevant is to look at the halt to the progress of India in telecommunications since 1991. That stunted progress is a tremendous economic and technological blow, far exceeding Sukh Ram's alleged 'makings'.

	1996 (over 1991)	
Items	**Production**	**Costs**
Switching equipment	+ 300-600%	- 50%
Telephone instruments	+ 60%	- 50%
Transmission system	+ 500%	- 65%

The table on page 69 shows production going up in various items from 60 per cent to 600 per cent, and costs coming down 50 per cent to 65 per cent. No other Indian industry has shown such results in so short a time. This shows what new innovative technologies can do, and all this was a result of foreign collaboration. In spite of being in a commanding position for thirty years, the Indian telecommunications could only give us shortages, bad service, higher and sometimes arbitrary and exhorbitant bills.

Even Mr. Deve Gowda as Prime Minister could not tell us where we shall go from here. Do we have to wait till the political corruption cloud of DOT is lifted? In the past, the system has never been able to bring home charges of corruption or misuse of authority — another aspect of the same stymied syndrome. Or can the government muster the will, install an effective Telecommunications Regulatory Authority soon, restore confidence and trust to transparent competition and clear, stable rules, and get on with the job? Till then, 'the subjects, bereft of understanding are carcasses full of straw.' Such is the repeated *Adi Granth* fate of the people of India at the hands of the men of straw in office.

If Mr. Deve Gowda wished to know 'What went wrong?' with the public road transport system, he did not have to step out of Delhi. The Delhi Transport Corporation (DTC) is a notorious case study of how a public transport system should not be run; whether it is the convenience of passengers, the horrendous accident rate inflicted on the public in terms of deaths and injuries with no legal action, the poor maintenance of the fleet of vehicles, or the shocking financial results of annual losses of Rs. 16 Cr. The heart of the matter in public transport is the same as in power, irrigation and ports — the lack of political courage in raising tariffs to meet viable costs, and mismanagement of staff. The DTC was corporatised twenty-five years ago. For twenty-five years this failure has been perpetuated. Monthly passes for students are sold at a paltry rate of Rs. 12.50, a rate probably valid in 1975. Free meals, free tickets, free water and power; that seems to be the answer of the men of straw, presuming to govern a country on which they inflict an average annual rate of inflation of about 10 per cent.

The *sirkar* has not only failed to govern, it is now indulging in a massive cover-up by writing off huge past losses of DTC — as also DESU and the Delhi Milk Scheme — by merging these in the Delhi government with nil liability after past losses! All these are centrally administered. This device, an administrative trick, does not change the realities of the situation at all.

Only 20 per cent of Indian roads are in good condition, compared with 50 per cent in Thailand and 70 per cent in South Korea. Another victim of *theka* raj and large misappropriations. In the Bihar bitumen scam, bitumen worth lakhs was billed, with no new road work. Most Indian roads are fifty years behind present and future traffic needs, and have become the new killing fields with huge accidents and losses of life.

Let's come to the blood-stream infrastructure of the economy, the banking system, behind which is the RBI. The nationalisation of the banks in 1969 was Mrs. Gandhi's political spear against Morarji Desai and the Syndicate, opposed to her in her Congress party. This was a populist, one-up-manship measure. *Garibi* or poverty was to be eradicated with the nationalised funds of the banks. So this Joan of Arc of India's poor millions set off on her populist crusade with that 'unconstitutional authority', Sanjay Gandhi and hordes of cronies in tow, leading to the imposition of the desperate Emergency within five years, and the breakdown of Indian democracy; followed by massive corruption, the Amritsar tragedy and her own assassination. The 'tryst with destiny' seemed to have run into a blood bath.

After the bank nationalisation, there was the first portent of Nagarwala, his sequestering Rs. 60 lakhs in cash from State Bank of India (SBI) with 'Mataji's voice', and his disappearance thereafter. This was only the tip of the ice-berg of public loot. But close on the heels of that, followed the trumpeted Loan Melas, with hordes of politicians using millions of depositers' money as another non-repayable giveaway, mainly to and through the farm lobby to be partly recouped into private and party coffers. Over 40 per cent of the public's deposits were ostensibly earmarked for the 'priority sector', the same Loan Mela carnival, with political patronage for advances, but no political responsibility for repayment of the depositor's money. As the years went by, the banks suffered increasingly from this looting with anaemia, doctored by inadequate accounting, capital inadequacy, RBI paper norms, and poor auditing. Appointments of senior bank managers followed the system's normal course, pliability and 'commitment', playing the game by the crookish informal, not the formal rules of the game. By 1980, the nationalised banks too were on the 'commanding heights', holding 93 per cent of the network of branches and 89 per cent of the loans.

In the Eighties the hard realities began to bite. In 1991 the banks made collective losses of Rs. 41 billion or US $ 1.2 billion; when the total international aid to India in that year was Rs. 11,615 Cr. or US $ 4.6 billion, with total debt servicing of Rs. 6,655 Cr. or US $ 2,720 million. In one year, 1991, the collective losses of PSU banks amounted to a staggering figure of nearly half the foreign debt servicing of India. Post-1991, the treasury had to pump in several thousand crores to ensure capital adequacy. During 1993-95 Rs. 10,000 Cr. were pumped in; in 1995-96 — Rs. 850 Cr.; in the current year (1995-96) Rs. 908 Cr. is contemplated. How long will these large endless doses of capital at the tax-payer's expense go on, in what was supposed to be a viable banking system, with enough resources to lift *garibi* as well! With rising costs and interest charges, with mounting non-performing assets (NPAs), the nationalised banks have made overall losses since 1992-93. Only three out of twenty-seven nationalised banks have had NPAs below 18 per cent since 1993-94; eight had NPAs between 20 per cent and 40 per cent, the depleted harvest of Loan Melas, political influence, and bad management. Norms have been flouted, unpaid interest and bad debts were concealed, and audits have been dubious. The auditors in their reports usually state: 'subject to our qualification, the accounts reflect a true and fair view.' The above operational failures are concealed from auditors, and the banks' reports on them are inordinately delayed; hence that caveat 'subject to our qualifications'. It really means the auditors were hinting to authority, Parliament and public, that the banks' accounts were not 'true and fair'.

At last a dissenting note has emerged from the auditor in the case of the bluechip Punjab National Bank (PNB), which shows:

— the bank understated its losses in 1995-96 by Rs. 146.23 Cr. declaring losses of Rs. 95.9 Cr. when it was actually Rs. 242.36 Cr.;

— this was a device to show capital adequacy over 8 per cent required by RBI;

— there was an overstatement of advances by Rs. 37.51 Cr., and an understatement of liabilities by Rs. 108.85 Cr.;

— there was an understatement of unsecured advances by Rs. 823.46 Cr., and an overstatement of secured advances by that amount.

If all this can happen in a reputed bank like PNB, one can imagine the magnification of this in the remaining twenty-six nationalised banks. The chronic cases of UCO Bank, United Bank of India, Punjab & Sindh Bank, and Indian Bank have ballooned. This raises the vital question of the regulatory capacity of the RBI itself, and the Department of Banking, Ministry of Finance. 'What went wrong' in these regulatory centres? Where was effective Parliamentary scrutiny and accountability outside the political motivations behind the Bank scam? The fault is not, once again, in the lack of law and rule, but in the capacity and character of the regulators of the system. After the Bank scam burst in the nation's face in the early Nineties, the Finance Minister attributed this to the same generalised 'failure of the system', which seems to put a neutral, non-accountable face on it. Harshad Mehta and company were only clever opportunists of systems which were inherently wrong. The PSUs were known to be failures for decades, yielding no returns on huge investments in the non-oil sectors, against Mahalanobis' promise to Nehru that they would be giving the nation profits in ten years! Profits which could not be seen even after thirty-five years! When public opinion began to be concerned, government gave the usual knee-jerk reaction to put pressure for profits, without any fundamental thought in the re-engineering of public sector management systems with real autonomy and clear objectives. So the PSUs took the easiest course of planting money on the banks for higher returns. The banks and the brokers then produced a major unnatural upthrust of the stock market, since described and investigated as a 'Scam'. India's stock exchanges have not recovered since, and equity investors have suffered and withdrawn. Three years have gone in tinkering, yet the Finance Ministry, RBI, and Stock and Exchange Board of India (SEBI) have not restored a major instrument of investment for growth, the Stock Exchanges of India.

Belatedly, public sector banks are now considering the performance criteria. Even in the list of these, one does not see the profitability criteria of bank branches anywhere; neither the units of operations nor clear customer service.

These criteria do not figure in the 'culture of the *sirkar*' pervading the banks. At the end of the day, these criteria should lead to profitability, and where they don't, branches can be clearly identified for remedial action from the bottom up. This is more so because regulation from top down has failed patently. As in the case of DTC, the merger of a failing bank with a more successful one is hardly a remedy. It is a plain cover-up and a hope and nothing more than that. Men of straw usually opt for the easiest way out; they cannot face and overcome problems squarely.

So what have the ruling men of straw learnt from this experience since the nationalisation of banks in 1969? Public opinion in a democracy must force them to learn. The first lesson is to act with transparency and integrity as the custodian of the public's resources and the depositors' money, which is not for the politician to play around with. The second is to ensure that regulators regulate and systems do not fail. The third is to ensure a strict control on bad debts and elimination of habitual debtors, especially those enjoying political patronage. Last, but not the least, customer service and profitability, and the end of frauds and Loan Melas. Or else, the *Adi Granth* points to 'carcasses of straw', littering the land with bankrupt PSUs, Centre and state, draining precious resources from social development in the critical health and education spheres, depriving 95 per cent of the people of these basic development needs for the benefit of the 5 to 10 million in the politician's 'milch cows' of the *sirkari* sectors. And when the pink and red keep calling this policy 'pro-people', they seem to have forgotten to count.

In contrast to the dismal results of public sector banks, and belying the glib assumptions of *swadeshi* ideologies afraid of competition, it is good to see the better performance of private sector Indian banks in the Nineties, even better than foreign banks; in growth rates, in deposits, in advances, in market shares and in income shares. Let there be more transparent competition, with autonomous management, effective regulation and audits, proper accountability, and no 'systems failures'.

Now, and in the twenty-first century, the most concentrated crisis of infrastructures will be in the cities and towns of India, where half of India will live after 2000 AD. India will then cross a political climactic. In the past fifty years, the majority of the electorate have been in vast dispersed rural areas. After AD 2000 they will be concentrated in the urban areas, a more vocal dynamic force, which will not tolerate the breakdown of infrastructure services easily. Yet, as of now :

— a quarter of the urban households are without toilet facilities, and people use streets, *gullies*, canals, rivers to defecate;

— only 18 per cent cities have partial sewage and treatment facilities;

— up to 30 per cent to 50 per cent of solid waste in urban areas is uncollected;

— 25 per cent to 50 per cent of the population of urban areas live in slums, and their growth is on the increase;

— in middling cities and towns 56 per cent have no access to tap water, 63 per cent are without toilets, 68 per cent without drainage, and 98 per cent without access to dustbins for garbage.

The question to be asked is why? This is so for the same reasons as have been shown so far — politicised inefficiencies, corrupt tax collection leading to heavy losses of revenues, and incapacity to invest in municipal infrastructures, a lack of transparency and public accountability.

Yet, Mr. Deve Gowda, the answer to all such problems in cities, states and at the Centre has been demonstrated in Ahmedabad by Sardar Patel at a political level, before Independence and by Municipal Commissioner, Keshav Verma, at the bureaucratic level since 1994. Ahmedabad was like India, a rich city with poor infrastructure. The municipal corporation had been in debt since 1983, with no capital works since then, and like most of India 85 per cent to 90 per cent of revenues went in salaries, a symptom of *sirkari* inertia. The plague of 1994 compounded matters.

Fortunately the hour and the place found their man, Keshav Verma, an excellent example to every municipality, state and Central governments. He began by clearing 75,000 tons of garbage, and won performance credibility for the Corporation and himself. Action spoke better than political manifesto or policy statements. In the face of the local mafia, he stopped criminal evasion at check points, and raised Rs. 100,000 per day in the first three months. In the past, he said, 'there was no moral courage to stop them.'

That, Mr. Gowda, has been at the heart of the failure of Indian politicians, the want of moral courage. He then cut off utilities for non-payment of dues, another ubiquitous source of the non-viability of all infrastructures in India. the Corporation began to collect outstandings estimated at US $ 200 to US $ 300 million. By 1995, in less than a year, the city's long-pending debts were erased. For the first time in Ahmedabad's history there was a surplus. As a result of the city's vastly improved financial health, it could now finance US $ 50 million. Ahmedabad's credit rating, never heard of before for a municipal corporation, was given as A+ in 1996 by an associate of Standard and Poors of the USA. Here was a highly commendable example to the rest of India in efficiency, transparency, accountability, and viability; with self-reliance and no dependence on state or Central governments. As to whether it would be sustainable after Verma goes, he himself said, 'Whether I go, it will continue. Because of the transparency and growing professionalism of the cadres, the system is not as vulnerable now to change in Commissioners.'

Similarly, in filthy plague-infested Surat, another public servant with moral courage, S.R. Rao, Municipal Commissioner, cleaned out the city's clogged drain pipes, removed months of accumulated mounds of garbage, reduced octroi and excise evasion, and transformed one of the dirtiest, disease-infected cities of India, into the cleanest in the country. This was declared so by the Indian National Trust for Architectural and Cultural Heritage. He did this by: (a) setting a personal example; (b) getting his officers to get out of air-conditioned offices and into the streets;

(c) giving them financial powers to sign cheques upto Rs. 2,00,000; and in the process his own daily file work came down from 450 to 80! When fines for litter were limited to only Rs. 50, he invested administrative charges upto Rs. 1.25 lakhs to clear garbage and polluting materials. He described his achievement aptly in a *desi* simile. 'When I came Surat's administration was like a fly trapped in *srikhand* — it could neither sink nor swim, but merely struggled in a single spot. I have helped this fly to escape. It is up to the organisation to find its wings and soar.' Hundreds of Municipal Commissioners, and thousands of public officials stuck like flies in the *srikhand* of India's infrastructures, can follow the exemplary roles of Keshav Verma and S.R. Rao. The test of politicians, promises and manifestoes lies in supporting such officers, and setting high performance norms, not parasitic ones.

Keshav Verma of Ahmedabad and S.R. Rao of Surat have lighted two significant candles for the rest of India, as to what can be done to change the multiple angst-ridden, politicised dysfunctional counter-systems created by lesser men in the last fifty years. Moral courage has made the difference in two of thousands of India's public servants. It would appear as if the Central and State Public Service Commissioners have ignored this basic criterion in the past. And so has the entire government structure.

Rape of the Indian Environment

Glowing economic reports are possible even as the economic policies that generate them are destroying the resource base.

Experience tells us that the ecological indicators of today foreshadow the economic trends of tomorrow.

— **Lester Brown,** *World Watch*

The community of development economics had earlier taken the world for a ride with facile notions of input/output models, with cheap oil, with misleading political promises doled out by politicians in Five Year Plans, and in India, a deteriorating implementation machinery of mounting costs. Meanwhile, signs of desertification are growing in India and many parts of the Third World, especially in Sub-Saharan Africa (the Sahel), with growing populations exceeding carrying capacities, and with high cost energy, unemployment, inflation and debts. The economies of many countries are ceasing to be sustainable in either economic, ecological, or social terms. Eco-stress has intensified social stress and uprooted millions of ecological refugees. To budget deficits have been added the far more threatening biological and agronomic deficits arising out of eroding eco-systems. Both deficits, of natural resources and of national finances amount to the politics of plunder, and forfeit all moral claims to the promotion of social justice, when rulers and planners are plundering the natural capital of our children and grand-children. All these symptoms of state and society collapse in Southern African states should serve as a warning to India. India's financial management may not be as profligate as that of South America; but a stage has been reached when the Finance Minister has admitted that the state is living off citizens' taxes and its reckless borrowings, and that development funds now have to come from huge borrowings, national and international. Beyond a point, which has been reached, the state's economic appetite for its own maintenance cannot be reconciled with its major *raison d'etre*, development. If those borrowings cannot be serviced, India falls into an African style debt trap; and then everything is in threat, democracy, economic development, even state government and civil society.

Barely a decade ago, the Leontief model for the UN projected a rosy economic future for the world till AD 2000, as did Mahalanobis in India in the Fifties. These prestigious exercises have proved to be just pies in the sky! They were the work of theoretical statistical economists. They lacked an interdisciplinary basis in which ecology is the core. They offered the politicians marijuana, which has now become 'brown sugar', a transition from unreal dream state to certain death, and at such high cost on land, water and in the atmosphere.

We must now learn from past lessons and take three major steps to create a new eco-development process. First, we must learn that eco-development failures, e.g., in deforestation, soil and water depletion, have been inherent in many development policies. We must change those policies, and manage the national budget as we would expect prudent householders to manage family budgets. Second, we must go back to the drawing board and re-examine the relationships of demography, ecology, economics, and engineering in all the major development problem areas, and evolve better interdisciplinary answers. Third, we must change over from the politics of paradise-promising and plundering, to the politics of productivity and sustainability, the preservation of life-support systems and the sustainability of natural resources. This will require a changed political and bureaucratic will, the will to face facts, to change disastrous trends, and not to live off the capital of our children. Development politics has got to stop fooling all the time. In that task, the media and public opinion have a crucial historical role to play in contemporary communications-managed societies. We cannot hope, wishfully, that the past politics of development will change on its own. 'What we need is a total vision of development,' says Avininder Singh of the Environment Committee of Confederation of Indian Industries. Indian politicians show no signs of any such conception, not one of them, from the Prime Minister to the Environment Minister.

More of the same — the usual promise of rising national budgets and deficits — is only sending bad money chasing after bad politics, a kind of Gresham's Law in eco-development. This leads to more desertification and social disorder; and with past neglect of social development expenditure it offers less development and less security. The bureaucratic tinkering with old processes will not do, nor will insertions of empty cliches like 'ecological balance' into plans which are destroying ecological life-support systems. Dr. M.S. Swaminathan, eminent agricultural scientist believes that 'extensive environmental damage now occurring due to human greed and indifference can be reversed. We need a cadre of development ecologists, who could help the country achieve the needed growth rates in income and employment based on principles of economic sustainability and social and gender equity.' Every eroded grassland, every felled tree, every drying spring or water body compels poor women to go further and work longer hours for fodder, fuel and water.

First, let us see how the past policies themselves have dug the present graves. Take the cities first, the 'unintended cities' as one architect has put it. There has been no land-use planning in constricted space being filled with squatter by rural migrating millions, from depleting rural hinterlands. Alternatively, Master Plans are subverted by the political-commercial complex, leading to speculative land deals, hyper land and property inflation, the pricing out of the poor and middle classes, the absence of sensible housing policies for these classes, uneconomic rent laws to make for economic housing expansion, and the growing cancer of slum growth with squalor, unhygienic living conditions, pollution and crime. The slums themselves then become a vast vote bank and a vested interest of local politicians, slum lords, smugglers and criminals. That is the road to the collapse of civic life, to mounting problems of conservancy, insanitation and disease, to acute housing shortages for all but the super rich, to power failures, to high-cost, imbalanced transport systems choking the streets and grinding down motor vehicles to the speed of cycles in city centres. Cities are becoming disease, crime, and early death traps. Yet these cities, the generators of wealth and now approaching half of India in size, are not on the political agenda at all.

After more than a decade of Calcutta Metropolitan Development Authority's efforts to save Calcutta, after expenditures of millions, it was found that the per capita consumption of water, power, and transport was less in the mid-Seventies than in 1951. It may well be so in other cities too. Half the populations of the metro cities in India live in slums and on the streets in these 'unintended cities', in a so-called planned economy. The festering, growing sores of the cities of developing countries could well be the graves of their governments in the twenty-first century, unless there is a firm reversal of all past policies and practices. By then, the cities will be the unbearable receivers of the flotsam and jetsam of rural populations, of which there has been ample evidence so far, as a result of the failures of rural development policies as well. The twenty-first century urban cancers will be the products of failed twentieth century rural and urban development, Mr. Deve Gowda.

There is only one hope, a strong political-cum-bureaucratic will to put urban India on the political agenda, to go back to the drawing board, and the politics of urban/rural settlement and planning now, beginning with more effective population and natural resource planning. The Central Cabinet and the Planning Commission need to commission action-oriented Task Forces for this purpose to plan afresh for the next fifty years. The Task Forces should be divided into the major agro-climatic regions and economic 'catchments', to take their plans closer to the realities of each region. Its work should be a priority item on the agenda of the four Regional Development Councils and the Planning Commission, and involve state governments and local urban administrations.

Consider the still vaster problems of rural areas, failure deriving directly and indirectly from development policies themselves. Whilst Africa is in an advanced stage of eco-stress, policies in India are following the same deadly path. One only has to look at the African countries to see what Sahelisation has done to eco-development, to the quality of life, to threats to the survival of states and civil societies themselves.

In this context, there is no early hope of population stabilisation with the present population policies either in India, Asia or in Africa, with the rare exceptions of Cuba, Thailand, and Indonesia. Projections of the World Watch Institute, Washington and the World Bank reports, show that India threatens to add half the population of China to its recent one billion people. Past policies have not been able to bring down India's annual population growth rate below 2 per cent, another of Nehru's blind spots, followed by Sanjay Gandhi's brash intrusions. He hurt the Indian sensibilities to such an extent that in complete contrast to even the authoritarian regime in Indonesia, it has made population planning a taboo subject for Indian politicians since. They are policies which have been erratic, low in priority, low in funding with too high a dependence on propaganda, too low on facilities on the ground, and a negligence of some major features accompanying successes elsewhere. These are : (a) a sustained political/bureaucratic will; (b) a wide range of effective social policies making for high rates of breast-feeding, delayed marriages, lower infant mortality, and higher women's education. Even family planning research is almost nonexistent. In a planning apparatus with weak goals and poor follow-up, population policies too have suffered. The people who relied on the 'trickle down theory' in economics, also relied on the mistaken belief that 'development is the best contraceptive' — both wrong assumptions, especially when social development itself has been failing. India's population policies in the last thirty years may be best described as a mix of superficial, weak and poorly-funded planning, and negligent or brash implementation.

It may well be said that the future of India will depend more on successful family planners than on successful economic planners. But where are they? There have been only a few inconsequential voices like that of J.R.D. Tata off-stage. In this sphere, Sanjay Gandhi destroyed courage in

Indian politics with foolhardy brash population-control measures. Rajiv Gandhi did not put this at the top of his 'political' priorities, with a wide political consensus among all political parties to bring heart and mind back into the core problem. It is too big an issue to be left as a side issue to a department of one ministry, with practically no social mobilisation beyond a few Non-Governmental Organisations (NGOs) at the state and district levels.

Take soil erosion, the basic shrinking resource base. But for the consistent voice of B.B. Vohra, soil conservation has been the most back-stage feature of Indian planning. Till the Third Plan, it was not even recognised. Since then Plan allocations would hardly fill the nation's beggars' bowls. Our measurements of soil erosion are at best guesstimates, with the most meagre investments, weak techniques and training, involving errors of judgement. The whole of the upper Ramganga catchment (Uttar Pradesh) measuring 1,500 sq. km has barely half a dozen measuring stations. The whole of our agricultural science world has no Erosion-Productivity Impact Calculations. (The loss of 3.9 inches of topsoil in West Africa cut corn yields by 52 per cent.) It is estimated from indirect indicators we lose 6 billion tons of topsoil from crop lands alone, more than twice the US level, apart from losing vast areas to salinity. In the US it is estimated a nationwide soil inventory would cost only US $ 30 million. If it cost half that much in India, it would be a very small price to pay, considering also that we have invested many times that amount in importing fertilisers and installing fertiliser plants. A fertiliser plant in every district of India would not compensate for the loss of

6 billion tons of topsoil every year. Yet we have not undertaken such a nationwide soil survey. Chauvinist tempers rose when China quietly took Aksaichin in Ladakh, where it was said, 'not a blade of grass grows'. The same chauvinist brigade is blind to the loss of 6 billion tons of rich topsoil.

Over forty years and many dams, our policies and planning have ignored the eroded upper catchments, and planned only for water and power downstream of the damsite, with the life and investments of those dams reduced between 50 per cent and 90 per cent in most cases. Every such dam is a failing non-renewable resource, apart from inefficient inequitable water distribution system, and the inhuman treatment of oustees.

India's soil policies have been almost totally absent. About half the landmass of India is unfit for productive cultivation. Its land reforms have lagged badly. Its consolidation of holdings in face of generational fragmentation has been dropped since 1947. With human and livestock populations doubling since then, we are an agriculture-bound nation with no land policies worth the name. We deserve the old saying: 'They that eat their soil, the soil eats them.' This is what the men of straw have fated us to in the last forty 'planned' years.

Take forestry policies. Despite the post-Independence Policy of 1952, Forest Departments have been practising the exploitative colonial policies since 1892, with one overwhelming ostensible objective, revenue, and another hidden objective — political funds. As a result forest cover has shrunk to less than 10 per cent, and in the Himalayan region good forest cover is less than 5 per cent; against internationally recognised needs of 30 per cent in the plains and 60 per cent in the hills. The old unholy alliance of forest contractor, politician and forester has denuded India's rich forest wealth of only a century ago, when 40,000 beautiful tigers found their habitat, now reduced to less than 2,000. Our politicians fail to see the symbiosis between tigers, wildlife, and human life leading to incalculable consequences for more soil erosion, water loss, land-slides, annual floods, and yet unresearched micro-climatic changes. Nowhere in India's agriculture and forestry planning is there a serious scientific awareness of what the millions of hillmen and tribals know; the very important energy flow between nearby forest and farm land for man and livestock. For every unit of farm land, there is a support system of 10 to 20 or more units of forest land, steadily degrading and reducing that energy flow of firewood, fodder and timber. Development planning has failed to address itself to this crucial energy flow; to minimise its constraints and maximise its potentials. Its face is turned the other way, towards revenue for the state and riches for its hangers-on.

For fifty years Indian forests have been frittered away with the customary rights and low prices of colonial times nearly a century ago. Local farmers have had customary rights to trees at rates fixed five to seven decades ago, under Rs. 5 a tree, when market prices have recently risen from Rs. 50 to Rs. 20,000 for different kinds of trees. The paper industry too has been permitted forest resources at concessional rates. Between farmers and industry, the

Forest Department has practised unrealistic low-priced policies, subsidising the rapid destruction of the nation's critical wealth for ecological health. The costs of this cheap exploitation have been incalculable. This is a clear and classic example of the politics of plunder, the major source of election funds in past decades in forested regions.

In all the constituencies where there have been forests in the past thirty years, ill-gotten forest wealth has been extracted to pay for the politician's elections, with massive connived corruption of officials and contractors. The new Forest Corporations have yet to demonstrate they are any less exploitative. Food and Agriculture Organisation (FAO) has indicated the following ratios of forest clearing to planting in the tropics, 1980-85. In India the true ratio is likely to be 20:1.

Ratio of Forest Clearing to Planting in Tropics 1980-85

Region	Clearing to Planting Ratio
Africa	29 to 1
Latin America	10 to 1
Asia	5 to 1
Tropics Average	10 to 1

Source : FAO, Forest Resources Division, Tropical Forest Resources, Forestry Paper 30 (Rome : 1982).

Deliberate forest firing to cut down more 'dead' trees has become an annual summer holocaust in the Himalayan region in the last decade or more. Yet, as a former Inspector General, Forests admitted, forest fires were knowingly under-reported. As a result, anti-fire measures were under-budgeted and under-manned. Every summer the remaining nation's forests are put to arson, with nothing done and no one brought to book by a forest bureaucracy which has multiplied manifold since 1950. Even the economic returns of the Forest Department's lands are the lowest of all lands in India tended by the hand of man. The productivity of India's forests is among the lowest in the world, with the usual *sirkari* malaise of under-pricing, non-payment, *sauda* and non-accountability.

Millions of accusing voices have risen against past forest policies, the source of the problems. In the face of rising public opinion, the new 1980 policy has been long in incubation. As it was more of the same, and worse, public opinion bellowed. The document has since gone into indefinite hibernation. Never has a policy been more incriminating in public eyes. Every passing year makes the ecological clock tick faster towards desertification in once richly forested and watered areas. The policy not only ignores public opinion and sound eco-development, it hardly cares for its own scientific data of rainfall decline in many places. Cherrapunji, once the place with the highest rainfall on earth, 546 inches a year, has come down to 370 inches. There are similar statistics in Kumaon, with micro-climatic changes which planners do not heed.

Now take water. India was once known as a hungry country. It is fast becoming a thirsty country with no coherent national water policy. Like the land, water is fragmented into many departments, ignoring the unity of nature's water machine. One department spends money on major and medium irrigation, a second on minor irrigation, a third on drinking water, a fourth on ground-water and so on, each ignorant of the total recycling machine, each functioning blindly in its own small well. There is hardly any coordination between agriculture and irrigation, or among all the departments involved in water-conservation, in what is man's oldest occupation since he left hunting; namely bringing farming and water together. Nor is there any coordination between the future of agriculture and long-term plans for ground water development, resulting in sinking water tables. Water rates are low and their evasion fraudulently connived at. We have little or no knowledge, and no working plans for the largest reservoir of the country, the Himalayan glacial system. We are blind to the drying and dying of Himalayan hill springs to the extent of 50 per cent to 70 per cent, and this has been the major perennial source of water in the past.

For low-cost agriculture, we have high-cost, high technology, dam-based irrigation systems. And they are left incomplete after these high costs, with no secondary, tertiary or field channel systems following through to the farmers' fields. We are profligate with engineering costs and with water use. As a result, we are losing lands the size of many countries to salinity and alkalinity. Ironically, the misuse of water has created increasing salinated wastelands.

If energy is basic for all development, rural and urban, especially in societies with extremely low energy consumption, the energy drawing board calls for major changes of priorities, investments and purposeful management. Jerome Weingart has rightly said, 'The gap between rich and poor is an energy gap.' Our politicians and economists have not seen this too. Nor are they able to see that energy is the life-blood of modern civilisation.

The first policy change is to redress the gross imbalance between urban/industrial and rural/agriculture energy investments and development efforts, totally ignored by political parties who claim, ideologically, to be pro-people. Which people? Only the privileged urban blue and white collar people, the pampered minority. In the Seventies, the Fuel Policy Committee report showed that in 1970-71, agricultural energy consumption was only 5 per cent of commercial fuels, whilst mining, manufacturing and transport used 89 per cent. The National Council of Applied Economic Research report on 'Rural Energy Consumption in North India' showed that the consumption of commercial fuels in India was 30 per cent (predominantly in urban areas), and non-commercial fuels 70 per cent (predominantly in rural areas). Upto 95 per cent of households were dependent on non-commercial fuels, wood, dung, and crop residues. Even in the farm sector, holdings upto 4 ha. consumed only 7 per cent of energy inputs; whilst those above 44 ha. consumed 83 per cent of energy inputs; with an ascending scale in between. Policy therefore needs a strong dose of energy equalisation, if the reduction of gross inequalities is a major objective of development, and if the vote-seeking politicians mean what they say.

The second is a more scientific approach to achieve optimum mixes of non-commercial and commercial energy inputs in the major agro-climatic regions of hills, plains, plateau, and coastal areas, with their varying needs, constraints and potentials. For example, firewood needs are about twice that of the plains (36 per cent) in the hills and arid regions (64 per cent to 67 per cent). Dung cake as fuel is used only 5 per cent in the hills, compared with 27 per cent in the plains and 23 per cent in arid regions. In the hills, hydel and wind potentials will be highest. The wind potential will be high in the coastal areas. Biomass potentials will be highest in the plains and hills. So each agro-climatic region will need its own optimum mix for the largest number of people. There is no such concept yet in rural energy planning, which is solely dependent on rural electrification, which is only a minor extension of urban and industrial electrification, and too costly for 95 per cent of rural folk. The trouble with the one-track rural electrification policy is that : (a) it has virtually excluded most other rural energy development; (b) *gobar* gas plants are too few and with poor maintenance; (c) smokeless *chulhas* are discarded by the people within a year, if not less.

Unlike the case of forests, where the problems can be traced back to a coherent though wrong forest policy, there is no national water policy. India's water taps are either malfunctioning or in wasteful flow. Again that road too is leading to desertification, to a widespread shortage of water for 0.95 billion people. What will happen when we race beyond 1 billion to 1.7 billion! Then, no Bhagirath can bring down another Ganga, not even those who play mythological roles on the screen, and then hoodwink the people as government leaders.

Like water, we have no integrated national energy policy. Like water, we have yet to exploit the enormous power potentials of the Himalayas. We have an amalgam of ad hoc policies for coal, petroleum products, hydel, nuclear and now a weak entry into renewable energy. Apart from rural electrification for irrigation and some lighting, there is no policy for an optimum mix of all energy potentials from regional natural endowment constraints and potentials, for example, for mountain, plain, desert and plateau regions, each with different needs and circumstances. It is of a piece with the complete neglect of energy flows for fodder and fuel wood between farm and forest lands. So energy planning and provision is predominantly for the urban, the rich, the industrial sectors. Power flows through the grid to the powerful and the nonpaying. As a result, it is high capital and high technology oriented. The virtual captive of the state sector, it is highly inefficient, wasteful of resources and unsustainable. The SEBs utilise only 30 per cent to 50 per cent of their installed capacities. Not only have they all made heavy losses, but also have lost the capital invested in them, and they make demands for more and more. And all the while, power cuts and power failures plague factories, farms, and homes, without hope of improvement. Power wastages vary between 20 per cent and 35 per cent. The vast power bureaucracy seems to have been incapable of mending its managements, or cleansing its augean stables.

As we do not have a coordinated energy policy, so we also lack a coordinated sustainable pricing policy for different energy sources. As a result, since the oil crisis of 1973, the poor man's rates for energy have risen more than 200 per cent faster than the rich man's. Cheap kerosene, diesel, liquid petrolium gas (LPG), naptha and fuel oil have distorted energy-pricing and imports have led to diversion of kerosene to transport, added to pollution and made oil energy sources as non-viable as power plants, public transport and irrigation.

Investing a pittance in renewable energy since 1973, in a subcontinent of such vast solar, water, wind and biomass potentials, authority has launched on the highest cost, most dubious source of all energy — nuclear. And at a time when, with few exceptions like France, the rest of the world is reducing its orders for nuclear plants because of high uncompetitive costs. Its costs have doubled every four years. In the West, its costs are 65 per cent more than coal-fired power, and 25 per cent more than oil-fired power. In Japan, average real construction costs have gone from US $ 350 per kilowatt in the Seventies to US $ 1000 per kilowatt in the early Eighties. Cold economics has done to nuclear power what anti-nuclear enthusiasts could not do.

But this is not so in India, where nuclear energy investments have not been reduced, in dubious company with Pakistan, South Africa, Argentina, South Korea and Taiwan, all others, mark authoritarian states pre-1990. In India, the public and Parliament do not know its total investments, its real comparative costs, nor its dangers in a society not too meticulous about safety, but meticulous about secrecy. It is under secret wraps. Yet the promise of its future contribution to the country's future power is relatively low, behind schedule, and its risks covered up from public gaze. Its enormous investments could be transferred to Himalayan hydel power in small and medium projects, to more oil prospecting, to more efficient coal-mining, to photo-voltaics — a great promise of the future with no risks, to a wide range of renewable energy technologies. The development of the people 's needs for energy would be far better served with these far greater cost-benefits. Here too is a field for an important independent Task Force of high calibre, capable of examining the nuclear and non-nuclear sectors with hard objectivity.

There is no vested interest elite like a scientific elite. They are the new witch doctors, resentful of open challenge, unsharing in their beliefs, jealous of their powers, secretive in their ways, all in the name of the new bureaucratic divinity and national security. A democracy cannot afford to exclude them from its scrutiny in the public interest of this and succeeding generations. Their magic worlds are too dangerous, too spendthrift. They are not life-sustaining; they are life-destroying, as nothing before has been. Again it is the same story. Problems, shortages, wastages, failures and misdirections of capital in a critical development area go back to the shape and substance of energy policy and its missing elements.

In all these development areas of the past, a common psychological thread runs through most development planners, including politicians, and that is the path of least resistance and highest cost; not necessarily more science. It has been the planning, by a technological political coterie, in which the beneficiaries have been the privileged top 10 per cent, with fading electoral promises for the rest. The path of least resistance comes in the planning in the office, not in the field; in confining plans to a single department or discipline, excluding interdependencies; in ignoring the eco-stress repercussions on the ground. This split-departmentalised planning is also more conducive to surreptitious corruption and pork-barrel politics.

The only long-term sustainable politics is in the long-term sustainable development of India's soil, water, and forest resources, to prevent the slow Sahelisation of this subcontinent, as in sub-Saharan Africa. We need to learn from Norway's Resource Accounting System since 1977 in natural resources, and to study ecological indicators with economic indicators, to price renewable and non-renewable resources realistically, to bank gene pools, and not make deserts out of one of the world's most well-endowed countries. This requires men of vision and steel, not of straw and cardboard.

What is the cost of this environmental degradation, which these men and women of straw, these heroic cardboard cutouts have made the nation pay? Here are some findings of a World Bank study by Brandon and Hommann, 'The cost of Inaction: Valuing the countrywide cost of Environmental Degradation in India'. The costs amount to US $ 9.7 billion, or Rs. 34,000 Cr. p.a., and these are regarded as underestimates. At 4.5 per cent of GDP in 1992, India's costs are higher than those of China with 300 million more people at 2.6 per cent of GDP, for Mexico at 3.3 per cent of GDP, and 5 per cent for East Europe, and less than 1 per cent for industrial countries. The largest share is that of the growing pollution of water and air of Rs. 24,000 Cr.; deforestation in foregone production costs Rs. 9,450 Cr. annually. Water pollution results in the highest health toll in the country of Rs. 19,950 Cr. p.a. or 59 per cent of total environmental costs. Health costs are highest in the three mega cities of Delhi, Calcutta and Bombay, followed by Ahmedabad, Kanpur, Varanasi and Agra. Delhi's excess air pollution kills 7,500 people prematurely every year, 5,700 in Calcutta and 4,500 in Bombay. Out of the 40,000 premature deaths each year in thirty-six cities one-fifth occur in Delhi. Over 30 million life-years are lost in water-related diseases in India. Here is a summary of the breakdown of annual environmental costs.

Surface Water Pollution	-	59 %
Soil Degradation	-	20 %
Urban Air Pollution	-	14 %
Rangeland Degradation	-	3 %
Deforestation	-	2 %
Tourism	-	2 %

These costs have never been disclosed in eight Five Year Plans. They are no concern of the political manifestos. Press and public are unaware of the enormous dimensions of this multiple problem. The loss of Rs. 34,000 Cr. p.a. is thrice the average annual defence expense budget of India in the decade ending 1990-91; and about twenty times the central expenditure on social services! The ruling classes are benighted blind men.

As Lester Brown of *World Watch* has reminded us, if these are the ecological costs today, can one imagine what the human and development consequences will be in future?

India, known as a spiritual country through the ages, needs to rediscover the traditional source of its spirituality in the forests, waters and mountains of India, now called sustainable environment. There is a clear choice between past life-destroying technologies and plans, and the heed for life-sustaining ones; more so with India's phenomenal population growth. In this harking back to India's life, culture and spiritual roots, perhaps one should recall that simple poet of the soil from Maharashtra in the sixteenth century, Tukaram. In one of his songs he says :

'O you who are swallowed by the world, preserve something true atleast ... Make haste and sow seed to increase your store of good seed. If you keep company with thieves you will lose everything.'

There, in the simple language of a man from the soil, one of a type you claim to be, Mr. Deve Gowda, is the essence of the messages of sustainability of natural resources and not to plunder them like thieves; or we will 'lose everything', and our children and grand-children will face waterless taps, dry deserts, and no forests. If ever there was a *dharmic* development area, it is this. Yet it is not a serious matter on the political agenda of even *Hindutva* parties, despite a vague reference to 'sacred responsibilities' in Bharatiya Janata Party's (BJP) manifesto, undelivered in practice where they have ruled. The Congress has been the main culprit. The Left politicians seem to think their children don't need to inherit soil, water and forests; ideology is enough. All political parties are ambivalent, saying one thing and doing the opposite for local profit. All are politicians of opportunities, not leaders of a nation. Can one expect spirit from straw and cardboard, or vision from the blind?

Sauda alias Corruption

Beware of false prophets who come to you in sheep's clothing, but inwardly are ravenous wolves. You will know them by their fruits.

— **Mathew** *7.15.16.*

Mrs. Gandhi's famous statement that corruption was a 'global phenomenon' was a one-third truth, a self-justification, a general theory of extenuation. The two-thirds unmentioned was that in India it is traditional and universal, and that in the last twenty-five years the fount of it has been at the top of the state and political apparatus. As a result it has become endemic in all that the government touches. I am indebted to a senior Congress MP in Mrs. Gandhi's time for the true indigenous word for corruption, *sauda*. I was defending a Secretary to Government against his attack on corruption. His reply was 'Moddie Sahib, *aap nahin jante. Is desh me har baat ke liye sauda.*' I thanked him for the true *desi* word.

Nehru began by threatening to hang the corrupt from

the lampposts. Political and public opinion, plus good parliamentary conventions obliged him to sack T.T. Krishnamachari and the then Reserve Bank Governor, H.V.R. Iyengar after the Mundhra episode. Soon Krishnamachari was brought back to the Cabinet as Finance Minister, and Iyengar — once his Secretary, was awarded the Padma Bhushan. There was no more talk about the lampposts. The message to his and other parties was a green signal for the future.

This 'global phenomenon' varies with culture and historical experience. Indian *sauda* has a long history in the Indian style of governing. Over two millennia ago, Chanakya described that phenomenon as 'fish swimming in water', natural and common. That style of rule combined political and proprietory power. The state is a means to patronise and to endow. The greater the self-indulgence — usually with those who serve him or are nearest to him — the greater the stature of the patron, the model at its best of a liberal patron king. It was a traditional *Jajman*, or authority-dependence relationship. In the *Arthashastra*, the royal monopoly and prerogative extended far beyond land revenue to the whole economic system of trade in commodities, mining and metallurgy, transportation, even the control of taverns and brothels, the stamping ground of spies.

Evidence from Dr. Bernier, a French traveller to the court of Shahjehan and Aurangzeb, and the annual reports of State Vigilance Commissions, seem to point to the fact that, in India, corruption has been a traditional phenomenon. Dr. Bernier wrote to Colbert, the French Minister of Finance in the seventeenth century. 'My Lord, in the East, the great are never approached empty handed.' The system of *nazrana* had a history of centuries, and although the name may be in disuse, similar practices in various forms may be permitted to continue in substance. Tradition has also given it the seal of universal acceptance. When it comes to petty payments for a number of routine functions, which is the duty of bureaucracy to carry out without payment, the common person feels the force of traditional and universal practice. 'Everybody does it' and hence, if 'I don't I will suffer.' On the official side, salary and Dearness Allowance payment is regarded only for *hazri* or attendance! As a result, the belief of its inevitability is added to the traditional and the universal.

Therefore, in such a society to be above corruption one is expected to rise to the lofty level of a 'mahatma' or sink in the process as a fool or a failure. Nothing in the education of the child, either at home or at school, and not much in the training and accountability of public servants has changed the traditional and universal acceptance of corruption. If anything, the child learns from the ways of the parents and the teacher in the very first test of life, the examination. They will see ways round it and through it. The end justifies the means. A certificate or degree is the objective and not good education, which may include a certain amount of character building. The child sees that all things in life are achieved by 'connections', or by an offering. Hard work or enterprise are not necessary or not enough.

As stated earlier, in the last twenty-five years, the fount of corruption has been at the top and now there is a counter-system of corruption at all levels — systematic, brazen, harassing. It is exercised by everybody from *patwari* to minister. From the ration card to a thousand official clearances to the price of a legislator or a public office, everything has a price. Even those who mourn a family member's death are not spared harassment for a death certificate. Every control point is regarded as a license to harass and take increasing sums of money, without discretion or principle. At least, Sitaram Kesri, Congress President has admitted 'the problem that most parties face today is that partymen collect money in the name of election fund, and do not deposit it with the party' (*The Times of India*, 29.9.96). He confesses 'Today's politicians are different,' a mild understatement. It would be interesting to take an inside view of corruption as conveyed in the factual report of a certain State Vigilance Commission a few years ago.

The first underlying theme is that much of corruption is regarded as 'traditional and generally acquiesced in by the rural population'. In this connection, 'speed-money' may be exacted from individuals and from groups in a village for pumps, power, irrigation, loan, and a number of government facilities or controls, with which the villager has to deal. In the police department, the report says, 'the pattern of misdemeanour is traditional, i.e., demanding a consideration from interested parties before initiating lawful action, or for desisting from taking such action'. In the Public Works Department, again there is the mark of tradition in 'the acceptance of expensive gifts from contractors for favour shown,' which leads to all sorts of abuses with piece-work and muster-rolls. Even in the Medical department, the record refers to 'the traditional misdemeanours of this department' in demanding and accepting fees for treatment in government hospitals, and even for a diversion of dietary supplies and medicines for the personal use of the staff. The latest opportunity in this department is over cash disbursements for vasectomy operations. The report says, 'There were instances of decrepit old men and underaged boys being operated on and the same person being shown as operated on more than once,' for the compensatory allowances. The traditionality of corruption seems, therefore, established beyond doubt in department after department.

As a compliment to traditionality, there is almost universal apathy. The Vigilance Commission's report makes this disconcerting disclosure. 'The major handicap of the Directorate in its operations against corruption is the apathy, if not the hostility, of heads of offices and departments.' In these circumstances, detection with sufficient evidence is extremely difficult. The whole system resists vigilance and corrective action. On the one hand, the report itself acknowledges that corruption has grown with controls, and where controls have been relaxed, e.g., in foodgrains, opportunities for corruption have been reduced. The problem, therefore, is about what sanctions can the government, press and public opinion bring to bear on a society, where corruption is regarded as traditional, universal and inevitable. What can be done in a society where there is no marked 'work ethic' for hard work and enterprise, where beliefs in one's democratic rights for legitimate purpose is not strong enough; where politicisation has increased opportunities for corruption and made effective action difficult. Over the years, the first promise of many new state governments has been 'a clean administration'; and it is the first to be forgotten, possibly because no one has really expected it or demanded it.

One of the heartening reminders of the State Vigilance Commission's report is that, where there has been active supervision and the close identification of senior officers with the responsibility and implementation of projects, the scope of corruption is less, and the projects are completed in less time and at less cost. This was also a feature of the pre-1947 administration, dropped soon after 1947, as I found in my early IAS experience. I was amazed at this natural reversion which became so widespread so soon after Independence. It seemed like a widespread reversion to the natural, the intrinsic, to a long past inside us. We seemed to slip back so easily; the beginning of the cumulative 'failure of systems' admitted by former Finance Minister, Dr. Manmohan Singh four decades later when the Bank Scam blew up in Parliament. This report is in contrast to the fact that the old inspection system has broken down; that senior officers are so 'preoccupied with formulation and implementation of planned schemes that they find little time for supervision and evaluation'; with the result that there is no effective top-level supervision any more. In contrast, we have the example of a certain major project in the state in the post-war years, where the chief engineer found time to spend one week every month at the project site personally supervising progress. As a result, large economies were possible under the piece-work and muster-roll system. Although corruption is probably a phenomenon of all societies, in India it seems to take away from a capability of the leadership in all walks of life to achieve its objectives. It defeats the ostensible objectives of government, i.e. development, social justice, and economic growth. There are other corrupt societies where leadership is able to achieve its objectives. Here, they seem to be instruments of mutual incapacitation. Witness the alarming failures of intelligence and of espionage in the very highest offices of President and Prime Minister in the eighties. Witness the stalling of the infrastructure. Witness the threats to security through politicians' *hawala* transactions and their links with the terrorists, mafia and criminals. There was the remarkable confession of a Mayor of Bombay, as honest a politician as one could expect anywhere in the world, who said he was unable to achieve anything because of the army of inspectors and clerks who fed on corruption, and created problems beyond his control. One remembers that Nehru, Patel and Prasad were Chairmen of Allahabad, Ahmedabad and Patna Municipalities, respectively, before Independence, and that Nehru and Prasad gave up these posts as being too difficult to manage. This was an early and clear indication of the man of substance who held on and was able to achieve successful work from the others. It is said that as Prime Minister, Nehru pleaded helplessness with the people around him. This, along with the T.T. Krishnamachari and H.V.R. Iyengar episode, was the root of the infection that has now spread so widely. None of these were lost on the shrewd politicians. Therefore, one of the most important implications of corruption is not only its morality, but also its dysfunctional effects at all levels of society and government. Grandiose plans, programmes and promises come to nothing because of the amoeba of corruption, for which there appear to be no effective antibiotics in this country.

The irony of the situation is that whilst there is a deep desire for that fine thing called social justice, that desire is not accompanied by an equally deep desire to remove corruption and inefficiency which come in the way of social justice. Social justice has meant more state socialism, which, in turn, has led to more controls and an extractive politico-bureaucracy in traditional ethos which Vigilance Commission reports say lead to more corruption. This is a vicious circle around the major urge of our society for social justice. Yet that desire for social justice is negatived by universal *sauda* and corruption. The National Institute of Public Finance and Policy authoritatively reports that :

— 25 per cent to 50 per cent of public expenditure on canals is siphoned off into private pockets;

— 50 per cent to 80 per cent expenditures on anti-poverty programmes are defalcated;

— apart from *sauda* of private taxation for every form of public service.

(**Source** : 'Ravages of Black Economy' by H.R. Khanna, *The Times of India*, 10.7.85.)

In other words, corruption is not a peripheral nuisance on the circumference of public affairs; it is a worm in the very heart of the apple. The paradoxical thing is that the public seem to want the new clean apple in the case of others, and the traditional worm in their own interest! That is at the heart of the problem in an undeveloped civic society. Ambivalence again and again.

Before we deal with the surfacing of the *Patalganga* of *sauda* in the last decade, let us remember its prime stimulus in the Indian polity with Mrs. Gandhi since 1969. In 1954, an American administration expert pronounced India to be one of the six best administered states in the world. This was due to two major factors. First, India inherited the best administrative machine from the British out of all ex-colonial countries. Second, the national movement and Gandhi threw up a few educated, public-spirited politicians, who had a certain respect for law and public standards.

Mrs. Gandhi came in with pronounced *sauda* politics with a radical, populist front, and the pretence of legislation making political funding illegal. In this she was a hard and consummate practitioner. Caught in the internal power struggle of the 'Syndicate' of the Congress, she introduced populist politics in a hungry society to gain political mastery. The market for jobs, education, money and power expressed that hunger. In that context, she cleverly exploited the market of emotions and envy in a series of populist measures, which later threw the floodgates of corruption and unprincipled populism wide open. She launched a political thrust against big business, stalled industrial growth in the early Seventies, broke the pledge of her father's government to the Princes and forfeited their relatively small privy purses. She nationalised banks on the specious rhetoric of *garibi hatao,* and opened them to incidents like Nagarwala's extraction of Rs. 60 lakhs in "Mataji's" name from the State Bank of India, Delhi; then to widespread populist Loan Melas and years of bad debts and a series of scandals leading to the Harshad Mehta Bank Scam; and the Urea case of the remittance of Rs. 133 Cr. by individuals close to a later Prime Minister, for which not a ton of urea was imported. She knew better than any other Indian politician at the time, how to exploit the hunger, the envy, the indignation of the masses for her own political ends. She rode Chanakya's chariot in a modernising democracy. She wished to be the sole and supreme *Jajman*. All, save a few brave spirits of the earlier generation like Jayaprakash Narain and J.B. Kripalani, became her clients. The epitome of that traditional sycophancy was none other than the Congress Party President, with his notorious "India is Indira and Indira is India". Here was sycophancy trumpeted by stooges at the highest level, far from civic, democratic politics of self-respect, if not dissent.

Once the floodgates were opened at the very top of the Indian government and society, *sauda* alias corruption surfaced by capillary action like soil salinity rising to the surface, in a vast network of illegal markets, and in the criminalisation of politics with the money of smugglers, black-marketeers, *hawala* agents and criminal politics. Secondly by the extensive abuse of power, by Comptroller Auditor General disclosures, by citizens' actions through the courts, and by an eruption of pork-barrel politics from Bofors to Snam Progetti, to the St. Kitts' forgery, to the Bank Scam, to the Urea and Bihar Animal Husbandry Department's loot, to the disclosures of Minister Sukh Ram's disproportionate wealth through the telecommunications business. The nature of these calls for a little elaboration in a polity which has known little or no public accountability. How did this cumulative eruption happen in the last decade, gathering force over the years? For here were men and women of straw and cardboard, who behind their specious politics of *garibi*, social justice, and national development had turned the governments of India, Centre and states, into a massive looting machine which has increasingly become the prime purpose of government. It has been a reversion to a traditional, feudal style of rule which combined political and proprietary power by ministers, legislators and the majority of officials, flouting the very laws, rules and regulations which they themselves made earlier. They were Nostradamus' 'rascals, rogues, and freebooters'.

Press and people say the root cause lies in the election funds in a democracy. I believe the root cause lies in deep historical and cultural factors. Chanakya did not have 'democratic' elections, yet he knew corruption as a widespread phenomenon in his time over two millennia ago. Four centuries ago, Dr. Bernier could not reconcile the lavish extravagance of the imperial court and the nobles of Shahjehan's time, with the abject poverty of the people. He attributed this shocking disparity to the loot in the imperial court and that of the nobles, and to huge expenditures on wars. And for many centuries, princes, *zamindars* and *taluqdars* knew no distinction between the political (the state) and the proprietary (the personal). Our politicians in a constitutional democracy have been behaving like those feudal princes, *zamindars* and *taluqdars* whom they sought to abolish, deprive or reform after 1947. Atavistic traits that have been ingrained long ago cannot be uprooted by paper constitutions and paper laws.

The political party and the politician begin their political lives with illegal acts and frauds. They have extorted fortunes from Indian industrialists — lately foreign ones too — in defiance of laws against political donations. Even when charitable institutions are required to file income tax returns if income exceeds Rs. 50,000 p.a., with the exception of the Communists, no political party has filed its returns under S. 139 of the Taxation Laws (Amendment) Act, 1978. And why should it be 'voluntary' for political parties when it is mandatory for the rest of the nation? The Supreme Court has directed the government to file an affidavit on noncompliance of tax obligations under S. 13-A of the Income Tax Act in force since 1979. The government and its Income Tax department have failed to survey or raid a single political party's office, though they make a song and dance in the press in non-governmental cases.

It is the same with nonpayment of rent of official quarters by ministers, legislators, and the gross misuse of official power in out-of-turn allotments of such accommodation by ministers to ex-ministers, ex-MPs, etc. Their dues run into millions of rupees. Outstandings on house dues were over Rs. 25 million on September 30, 1995. There were over 9,000 out-of-turn allottees. About 30,000 official quarters have been sublet. Another 10,000 allottees have been given loans at public expense to build their own houses, while they continue to occupy and do not pay for official quarters. If all these allottees were evicted, about 49,000 quarters would be available for those who have had to wait fifteen to twenty-eight years of service to get housing. And this is the state of affairs in Delhi alone.

Grabbing land and property takes us to the latest emerging phenomenal manifestation from the land of political heroes and heroines made of cardboard cutouts. The Phillipines had one Imelda Marcos who amassed wealth as the President's wife. Tamil Nadu has thrown up two Imeldas, Jayalalitha and her mysterious companion Sasikala. With coercive muscle and underpriced money power — apart from the Mughal wedding of a foster son — 100 rich properties have been identified (25 in Chennai and 75 in the rest of the state), which appear to have been acquired recently, in just a few years of Jayalalitha's notorious reign. The value of a few of these add up to over Rs. 11 Cr., plus a 400 acre papaya land on the Tamil Nadu/ Andhra Pradesh border. An amazing success for a lady (Sasikala) who started with an ordinary video cassette shop in Chennai. This is apart from the chargesheets against Jayalalitha under the Prevention of Corruption Act for wrongful loss of over Rs. 3 Cr. to the state government in the acquisition of TANSI land in 1992. A loan of Rs. 1.5 Cr. for this land was sanctioned by the Indian Bank in one expeditious week! Another classic example of the blatant misuse of public office, the magnitude of which has yet to unfold, as in the multiple Bihar scams before and in the regime of Laloo Prasad Yadav. Both their regimes in Tamil Nadu and Bihar have not been known for good government, good development, or the alleviation of poverty. Personal aggrandisement seems to have gone with the running down of the apparatus of good government, and a depletion of state resources, and the misuse of bank funds. 'Unearthing of an Empire', *The Week*, 10.11.96 and *The Times of India*, 16.11.96.

The mass transfers of officials is another widespread abuse of power. Every post in government has a price. The makings are incalculable. CAG does not go into it; it is a political prerogative. Recently, the Supreme Court found two ex-cabinet ministers of the Central government misusing power by allotting petrol pumps, gas agencies and shops on government land to friends and relatives. We are Indian politicians please, this is our traditional patronage, no modern accountability or new-fangled 'judicial activism'!

Let us turn to the gargantuan capillary action of *sauda*, floating to the surface in the lives of millions of people; and these are only indicative at a point of time in 1994. In that year, there were 112,00,000 people waiting for LPG connections. The mean pending time was twenty-nine days, and the mean total cost (including gas delivery man, regulator and cylinder installation, forcible sale of gas stove, ISI marked) was Rs. 1,500 in each case. So, the capillary action involved something of the order of Rs. 1,68,000 lakhs in this one facility. Next, the mean unofficial cost of each passport varied from Rs. 10,000 to Rs. 23,000 to receive it on time. If we take the mean figure of the latter, or Rs. 16,500, the makings on every 1,000 passports was about Rs. 165,00,000. The illegal procedure for a driving licence involved a mean time of 140 minutes and a mean cost of Rs. 690. The illegal procedure for telephone connections involved a mean waiting of a month, and a mean cost of Rs. 15,000 via real estate agents, and Rs. 1,100 in illegal transfers from Khurshed Lal Bhavan to linesman. (Source: Bibek Debroy, *Business India*, 29.8.94-11.9.94.)

If we knew the total number of passports, driving licences, and telephone connections, the total illegal costs would amount to hundreds of crores on the make. And this is only a fraction of the total picture, which excludes untold amounts involved in transactions of land, property, octroi, licenses, permits, hospital, school and college admissions, ration cards, etc. The parallel economy of *sauda* could be a sizeable proportion of the formal economy of the state.

Next, let us take a look at three of the thousands of CAG disclosures over the years, again only indicative. First, the facts, before we come to conclusions.

In Himachal Pradesh, the CAG report presented to Vidhan Sabha for the year ending 31.3.93 showed :

— in spite of an expenditure of Rs. 143.35 Cr. on construction, and Rs. 142.03 Cr. on maintenance of rural water supply schemes, it has not been able to supply safe drinking water, with shortfalls in chemical and bacteriological testing of drinking water ranging from 89 per cent to 100 per cent of cases, and no bacteriological analysis of water in 777 schemes;

— 54 water supply schemes estimated to cost Rs. 434 lakhs were completed at double the cost of Rs. 909 lakhs, with cost overruns ranging from two to twenty-one years.

— 40 schemes were incomplete between 1973 and 1989, or over sixteen years despite an expenditure of Rs. 330 lakhs;

— while the state government had targeted to provide potable water to 11,887 problem villages in the Seventh Plan, 1,151 villages had not been provided with it till 1993.

All these wastages, delays, cost overruns and non-performance point to widespread and incalculable misappropriation of public funds in public projects apart from its enormous burden on inflation.

CAG found similar performances in the Madhya Pradesh Electricity Board. After spending Rs. 812 Cr. over six years on village electrification, CAG disclosed :

— only 67,238 villages were electrified out of a total of 70,883, or a shortfall of 3,645 villages, and there were no streetlights in 43,355 villages, or in 64 per cent of the villages supposed to be electrified;

— although a return of 10 per cent to 25 per cent was envisaged, the board suffered a loss of Rs. 2,538 Cr. in six years;

— only 980 pumps could be energised against a provision for 1,980 pumps, or half the number, with below target performances for single-point connections, street and domestic lights, and industrial connections;

— against a total provision for 3,680 schemes due for closure by March, 1994, only 3,193 schemes were closed, or a shortfall of 487 schemes; but expenditure was Rs. 2,153 Cr. against a provision of Rs. 1,443 Cr., or an overexpenditure of 49 per cent.

Here again, budget provisions are meaningless in terms of foreseeable reliable costs; there are huge shortfalls in performance but gross overexpenditures. The only conclusions can be inefficiency, corruption, and a complete lack of financial control or discipline in government with public money. Both the above examples of technological performance are in a country which claims to have the third highest technological and scientific manpower in the world. Our misappropriation capability must also rank very high.

The third illustrative case is that of a decade's continuous fraud and embezzlement by the Bihar Animal Husbandry department, said to be of the order of Rs. 950 Cr. or more. The main facts of the case are given below.

— In February, 1990 CAG addressed the Financial Commissioner about 'chronic delays in accounting for transactions may give rise to malpractices.' Against the desired monthly completion of accounts in the district treasuries, delays had extended from five to sixteen months.

— As the situation failed to improve, CAG held discussions with the Chief Secretary in May 1993 and February 1994. It was also brought to the notice of the Chief Minister

Laloo Prasad Yadav. But he sat on the file from 1.5.95 to 1.2.96, according to CBI sources.

— With increased delays, excess withdrawals increased as well.

— This was a collective failure under the rules of the Bihar Treasury Code all the way up from Treasury Officer, to Collector, to Commissioner in failing to inspect and correct. Fraudulent bills of huge amounts were being continuously passed by Treasury Officers, sometimes even without the required signature of the appropriate officials in the district offices.

Here was a labyrinthine statewise network of continuous and colossal embezzlement of public money by politicians and officials manipulating the entire administrative apparatus, even after years of CAG's factual reports and warnings of malpractices. The whole system of law, rule, inspection and accounting was undermined.

Multiply the above three indicative cases a thousand times, and one may have some idea of the enormity of fraud, embezzlement and corruption in the country as a whole. If Rs. 950 Cr. is systematically taken out of government treasuries, one can visualise the dimensions of the sharing network (unofficial *batwara*) among ministers, politicians, and officials. What may be good for the Laloo Prasad Yadavs in politics, is certainly not good for India.

Now for the notorious scams — these themselves only revealed the tips of the icebergs of massive *sauda*. They have accumulated and come to a head, thanks to the vigilance of the press and the writ petitions of conscientious citizens in the courts. It may be desirable to list the major cases to bring them to the nation's attention, as they are not occasional occurrences, but an ongoing widespread phenomenon, which has poisoned public life, and deprived the politicians, legislatures and governments of all credibility. It is not a few who are on trial; the entire nation is on trial in the magnitude of these revelations. God knows what is yet to surface.

Scam	*Unearthed*	*Approximate Amount (Rs. Cr.)*
Bofors	1987	63
Snam Progetti deals	1980s	?
Securities Scam	1994	5000
Sugar Scam	1994	650
Housing Scam	1995	17.4
Hawala Scam	1995	65
Jharkhand Mukti Morcha Bribery Scam	1995	3
Urea Scam	1996	133
Medical Equipment Scam	1996	1000
Telecom Scam	1996	1200
		Rs. 8131.4 Cr

(Source : KBK Infographics).

The enormity of these offences, these huge public frauds by public men at the highest levels of government are not confined to the individual or total amounts of money in only these cases. They are significant and dangerous for the following reasons.

— They undermine good government, economic growth, the security of the country, and a healthy democracy.

— This magnitude of brazen corruption has demoralised a whole society with continuous high inflation.

— The Bofors case has had a confidence-damaging effect on later defence purchases. (Rajiv Gandhi thought it impertinent to include the Prime Minister in the Lok Pal bills.)

— The stock exchanges of India have not yet recovered, even after three years, from the Securities Scam, damaging public savings and investments in the whole range of public and private enterprises since.

— The *Hawala* Scam not only blots the copybook of nearly all political parties, but is an indication of how Central Cabinet ministers can give shelter to anti-national terrorists and the mafia in state guest houses, damaging internal and external security. (It was during the suspension of *hawala* investigations that the Babri Masjid demolition, the Mumbai bomb blasts and communal riots occurred.)

— The Bihar Fodder Scam illustrates the total and systematic breakdown of administrative systems in conspiracies between politicians and officials of all levels.

— The Jharkhand Mukti Morcha (JMM) Scam not only illustrates how anti-defection laws are defied, but also the reality through political *sauda* of the whole political system of Parliamentary democracy, involving no less a person than the Prime Minister and ex-Central Cabinet ministers.

— The Medical Equipment Scam shows how, even in schemes aimed at the poor in hospitals and charitable institutions, a Central Cabinet minister, Director General Health Services officials, and the Customs officials were involved in dubious imports of medical equipment, which the People's Union for Civic Liberties estimates as a loss of Rs. 7,000 Cr. to the government.

— The significance of the Telecom Scam is more than the taking of illegal commissions — again alleged at Central Cabinet level. The significance lies more in the damage caused to the nation by slowing down telecommunications growth — so essential for modernisation and exports.

— The most brazen of these is the Urea Scam, in which Rs. 133 Cr. seem to have speedily gone out of public funds through public banks for unnecessary import of urea, not a ton of which has landed in India. Again, the alleged involvement of relations of a Prime Minister himself is a most serious matter.

It is not as if the private sector or the wider Indian society is blameless. Far from it. They have been equal instruments of *sauda*, venal politics and public fraud. Indian companies appear to have financed the buying of Jharkhand MPs in the JMM case. But their capacity for national damage is far less, and their legal vulnerability is greater. The government machinery can and has been mobilised into action as in the Bank Scam and numerous Income Tax raids. In the case of political and government malpractices, the official and political machinery provides the most effective cover-up, with long delays, and hardly any single significant conviction yet, as in Italy or South Korea. Corrupt Indian politicians have found that the best defence against law is the dilatory law itself; e.g., A.R. Antulay, Bangarappa, Nar Bahadur Bhandari, Arjun Singh, et al. Delay gives time for machinations and even a return to office. Latterly, there is even a stout pursuit of anticipatory bail. Durable politicians then have a way of suddenly developing cardiac, diabetic and other health problems.

Being made accountable after forty years of malpractices, politicians are now beginning to complain of 'judicial activism'. What they forget is that : (a) they are accused of violating the laws which they themselves have made, for which there should be the same accountability as for any citizen as no one is above the law; (b) in most cases it is the 'activism' of citizens and the press in a democracy which has initiated anti-corruption judicial processes; (c) the judiciary is only performing its role according to the Constitution and the law, which all citizens, political parties and governments should respect; (d) the supremacy of Parliament or the legislature does not arise in the culpable behavior of its individual members; (e) quite apart from the respective roles of legislature, executive and judiciary in a balance of powers under the Constitution, public figures in a democracy have to face established facts with constitutional responsibility, and be accountable under law. Or else constitutional democracy is subverted. The alternative to 'judicial activism', politicians should note, is the burning down of the house of a political kingpin of the Animal Husbandry Scam in Jehanabad, Bihar, by an extremist. Which do they prefer, 'judicial activism' or non-judicial summary destruction? Besides, politicians should know that judicial activism arises from citizen activism for citizens' rights under the Constitution.

Because of atavistic tendencies of the rulers to be arrogant and unaccountable, to ignore scrupulous distinctions between the political (the public) and the proprietary (personal), the problem of *sauda* has assumed alarming proportions, threatening the security, stability, and civic ethics of the entire Indian society. So, India is being treated to what Dilip Raote has described as 'the dance of the harlots', in the politicians' insatiable lust for power and wealth (*The Economic Times*, 23.8.96); and the sad, marked absence of a strong public opinion outside a few cities like Bombay and now Delhi. Recently, there have been signs of a healthy change in citizen awareness. It has to be seen how far the mass of the electorate really want a clean apple, without the corrupt worm of *sauda* in it. That clear choice will call for a radical departure from traditional ambivalence and behaviour.

Fortunately too, global public opinion is growing in issues like human rights, environment, ethnic minorities, and now even in corruption, which is being recognised as standing in the way of economic development and international business. Launched in 1993, 'Transparency International' is a coalition, in cooperation with World Bank and IMF to curb corruption. In its three years study, India stood among the three most corrupt countries with Pakistan and China, the work of men with no capacity to build institutions, only their private wealth and power. In the end, they are destroying the nation and themselves. National *sauda* has become a national disease.

The marriage of widespread political corruption and mafia crime has a telling historical impact in T.V.R. Shenoy's 'Return of the Pindaris' in *The Week*, 23.3.97. He reminds us that Governor-General Lord Hastings wiped out the widespread plundering Pindaris with a pincer movement from Bengal, Gujarat, and the Deccan in six months in 1817. It took his successor, Lord Bentinck three years to wipe out the Thugs by 1837. As at present, the Pindaris and the Thugs were 'abetted by local Chieftains for a price'. Admittedly, Hastings and Bentinck did not have to get elected by the people of India, but the Directors of the East India Company in London were never happy to spend money as good merchants, whether on anti-Pindari or anti-Thuggee operations, or even on the construction of the Upper Ganges Canal. But Hastings and Bentinck knew good government, and they demonstrated political will, which post-Independence politicians after Sardar Patel have dismally failed to know or do, despite the Vohra Committee report on the criminal-politician nexus. Shenoy concludes : 'The Pindaris, in independent India, have not just reappeared. They have occupied the chair of the Governor-General himself!'

Internal Pindari raj is the biggest single threat to the economic development and security of India. If Bihar and Uttar Pradesh are replicated in more states, India may look like sub-Saharan Africa. Let us now forget that these two states and Madhya Pradesh were the home of the Pindaris and Thugs, now called the 'Hindi heartland', the leadership of which shows no sign of curing itself. The politics of the Laloo Prasad Yadavs poses the fundamental democratic question to the state and to the people of India : is the contemporary politics of Shenoy's Pindaris 'pro-people?' Sooner or later, the electorate has to decide.

Public Accountability in Indian Polity: The Last Straw

For politicians, passing laws is like passing water. It all ends down the drain.

—**Rohinton Mistry**
in *A Fine Balance.*

Mistry's *A Fine Balance* is regarded as an epic of tragic realism. Public accountability in the Indian polity, hardly an epic, is a pathetic story of tragic realism too.

On the face of it, public accountability may seem a non-political, professional, administrative subject. This is totally wrong. We shall see that politics and historical and cultural factors are the primary determinants of the polity, which then influence society and government in the quality of public administration and accountability. One sees clear connections between aspects which affect public accountability in the polity in the African experience in an article by Jennifer A. Widner, 'States and Statelessness in Late Twentieth Century Africa'.* She shows those links with 'failed' and 'collapsing' states, a lesson for India. So public accountability in the polity is fundamental to the creation of good statehood, without which there is anarchy; as in Rwanda, Zaire, Angola, Chad, Ethiopia, and Sierra Leone, where even civil society does not exist.

While South Asian governing classes and elites have believed there is a wide distance between themselves and those 'failed' or 'collapsing' African states, no less a person than Dr. Mahboob ul Haq (ex Finance Minister of Pakistan), of the World Bank and United Nation Development Project, has cautioned South Asian states that they are heading for a sub-Saharan standard of living, with inadequate investments in health and education and with high armament expenditures. In fact, some African countries like Botswana, Côte d'Ivoire, Senegal, Zimbabwe, Gambia, Lesotho, Tanzania and Zambia have comparable and higher rates of investments in education and immunisation of children, than in South Asia between Indonesia and Pakistan.

Widner conveys effective government (the first concern of public accountability) equals efficiency and responsiveness. Her analysis shows marked and dangerous similarities between 'failed' and 'collapsing' African states and recent India. They are :

— low institutional performance;

* *Daedalus*, Summer, 1995.

— low return for the public from public expenditure;

— predatory behaviour of both ruling classes and mafia warlords;

— ineffective control of public expenditures and a narrow tax base;

— low spending on social development, health and education;

— widespread corruption;

— ethnic politics;

— weak intelligence enterprise, public information, public media and intellectual monitoring;

— bureaucratic immobilism; and

— governments overreaching beyond their capacities to manage, especially in enterprise.

India shares all these failures, to a lesser or a greater extent, in state-building. They are closely related to public accountability, which is widely acknowledged to be missing in India with all these marks of 'failing' states.

First, let us examine thirteen specific facts about the problem in the Indian polity and in Indian society, and try and assess the likely reasons for the lack of accountability in each case. We may then come to some factual and sociological conclusions in the later part of this chapter, which may then throw light on the deteriorating aspects of government, polity and society.

The first historical reason, so completely ignored by political scientists, is the obvious lack of experience in the management of the Indian polity for about two hundred and fity years between the end of effective Mughal government with the death of Aurangzeb and Independence in 1947. We forget that it took Europe over five hundred years to establish the basics of modern states with legislature, judiciary, a civil administration, a banking and financial system, and a standing army. A lot of social experience had to go into it at the state and local government levels, and in all organs of society.

The second historical reason, is that the Indian National Congress, the inheritor of the Indian state in 1947, did little or no hard homework beyond superficial annual resolutions for the needs of the future government in modern times in the world's most pluralist society, between 1920 and 1947. Between three incompatible models, Gandhi's Ram Rajya, the Westminster model, and the inheritance of a colonial structure of government, the future needs of a modern state and a civic society seemed forgotten. Intellectuals of that time seemed engrossed in India's past 'glories', as perceived, wishful or real.

Ironically, whilst rejecting British rule, the government of India, Centre and state, readily took over structure, legislation and controls from British colonial times. As far as public accountability goes, the major historical culprit has been the strong attachment to the British Official Secrets Act of 1923, which our politicians and bureaucrats failed to see was in conflict with Articles 19(1)(a) of the Constitution since 1951. It read: 'All citizens shall have the right to freedom of speech and expression,' in which 'information' should have been included. The Supreme Court has laid down that the right to information is part and parcel of Article 19(1)(a). A new Official Secrets Act has been enacted in 1989. But the long colonial tradition of secrecy, and a lack of public accountability of the previous sixty-five years has been a powerful anti-democratic and anti-public accountability factor. It has been carried to such ridiculous lengths on the security front in a satellite age, as to disallow Indian citizens from possessing Survey of India maps of their own country, and even the photographing of inconsequential little culverts. Such ridiculous secrecy is a mark of state paranoia, which is hardly a healthy condition for open government and public accountability. This explains the twenty year delay in the Janata Party's decision for more autonomous media corporations of All India Radio and Doordarshan. They are virtually the publicity agencies of ministers in office, with neither good news coverage, nor public accountability in vigorous open debate. There is no Right to Public Information Act yet. The word 'information' should be added to Article 19(1)(a) for that right to materialise.

The second example of a lack of public accountability, is the ambivalence of the polity, government and people, in the delusion that, once a problem is tackled by legislation it is solved, and there is no need for accountability thereafter. The ancient Brahmanical belief in the Word, Logos, *Vak*. This has been so from the earlier Sarda Act making child marriages illegal, to the constitutional provision for free compulsory primary education in ten years, which has been ignored; and to the representation of the People Act limiting election expenditures, and requiring accounts of political parties to be kept, which too was ignored before T.N. Seshan became the Chief Election Commissioner. The whole of Indian society, including the Income Tax department have connived at the failure to implement the electoral law of the land. If the law makers begin their political lives at election time with a public lie, with an open disregard of public law and integrity, how can one expect these legislatures to get honest accountability from governments, which is one of their primary functions? The electoral law has come to respect accountability only in the Seshan era. It remains to be seen if there is a lapse to the past after Seshan, a major challenge to Indian public opinion and the judiciary, one affecting the whole future of Indian democracy, politics, and the quality of public life. Government's direct accountability has recently been thrust on the Supreme Court by a few civic citizens.

Down To Earth, an environmental publication conveys another example of ambivalent *hukumat* in 'Clear Concepts, Unclear Courses'.

Ecological guidelines and policies are often not specific enough. Most of all, the professional class, in and outside governments, have not shown how to reconcile the interests of the ecological environment, and those of economic development in specific terms. Often there are no clear black and white choices. The famous Narmada dam is itself a good example. A recent proposal has shown how, even with a lowering of the height of the dam, the major objectives can be achieved, reducing costs significantly, reducing the flooded area by half, and with far less adverse effects on oustees. Anti-pollution technology, when installed at the start of a project, is less costly and more economic. Many environmental problems lend themselves to solutions combining economic development with : (a) more efficiencies in the use of natural resources and power; and (b) responsiveness to the needs, wishes and responsibilities of local people. What is often exhibited is a combination of short-sighted political opportunism, rigid technocratic attitudes, and a lack of real trust in, and partnership with, the people, ending up with corruption and inefficiency. In such situations, public accountability takes a back seat, until there are confrontations between authority and the public, either in the courts or at site. A heartening example of the latter is that of the people of Beawar, Ajmer district, Rajasthan. They have compelled the state government to recognise their right to information in all local panchayat-run development projects, including bills and vouchers against expenditures.

A third example is the lack of public accountability for crime. Earlier there was police indifference or neglect, no less than the failure of the public in giving evidence and in giving civic support to the police especially in communal crimes. Both the public and the police were weak in taking public responsibility for crime, including murder and dacoity. Over the years the growing hidden nexus between politicians and criminals, even Terrorist and Disruptive Activities Act (TADA) terrorists, has mushroomed into a subterranean labyrinth threatening India's security. Bombay was bombed over three years ago, and there has not been one conviction yet. Now the Central Bureau of Investigation (CBI) has charged a Central Cabinet minister of giving shelter in official guest houses to TADA terrorists. The Vohra report seems to provide evidence of widespread criminalisation of politics, but no names and no actions. Lesser evidence in Watergate led to investigative journalism which toppled a President in the USA. We have yet to see anything similar, even at lower levels. The investigative journalism done in the Bofors case has not been used to uncover and bring to book anyone yet, after more than eight years. The forgery of St. Kitts, the wiles of godmen in politics, and the admitted dubious role of the then Foreign Minister, have yet to be clinched, as in the case of the Bank and Sugar Scams. With this retrospect, the public have no confidence that the law will take its course, as the former Prime Minister promises in the latest *hawala* cases. There is an on-going cover-up of this growing cancer in India's polity and public life, largely through political guile, partly through a sufficient lack of moral indignation, partly through political devices like the Joint Parliamentary Committee on Bofors, and partly through the absence of strong investigative journalism in a culture of the *sirkar*. Indian society seems to relish scandals, decry corrupt practices, and play the role of an articulate spectator, all as an ineffectual pastime. A few public-spirited writ-petitioners of the highest courts are now changing the past complaisance.

How can one forget the terrible Bhopal tragedy, and its shameless exhibition of government's poor accountability, indifference, and even a venal trait in wanting to cash in on the compensation to be paid in dollars? In the process, it shamelessly proclaimed the inadequacy of the Indian judicial system in America, with not a single protest from the hordes of Indian lawyers and judges. It came to a belated deal with the American company after years. The lowest priority has been given to thousands of tragic sufferers, with belated, inadequate, or no compensations, and a callous attitude to continuous mass human suffering over a decade. Surely, the state and Central governments were equally culpable in the tragedy, in agreeing in the then Industrial licensing process, to locate the chemical plant so near to the densely inhabited areas in Bhopal. What were Factory Inspectors doing in the months preceding the disaster about apparent poor maintenance? Again, even a then concerned public and press were unable to get public accountability from a dominant government in that culture of the *sirkar*, where the public is secondary and hardly counts. Why has there been no sustained pressure of accountability in Parliament or the Madhya Pradesh legislature with such sustained suffering?

The world's largest industrial disaster was a clear indication of the prior joint culpability of governments, and the prolonged heartless attitude to thousands of poor sufferers, a heartless test case of a democratic government's public accountability. Did the media find itself incompetent to pursue the scientific and medical aspects of the case, apart from ensuring the minimum avoidable suffering and maximum feasible compensation paid timely? A decade later, Bhopal is almost a forgotten story, but a telling commentary on one tragic episode of this society's and its government's failure in public accountability in all its limbs, not least, the legislatures which are supposed to represent the people's interests.

Big dams, notably Narmada and Tehri, are a fifth specific example of poor public accountability, where the politicians and technocracy of four states have both refused to face techno-economic facts and, as in Bhopal, have been indifferent to the major and recurring human failure in satisfactory resettlement of oustees. Nor have they shown sufficient regard for environment, and in the case of Tehri, possible seismic dangers.

First, the politicians of all the parties in Gujarat took the people for a nebulous, if not a false ride, that the waters of the Narmada would irrigate all regions of the state, and convert it into a rich paradise. The nation can judge from former Prime Minister Rajiv Gandhi's telling admission that, since 1950, 80 per cent of the benefits of major irrigation envisaged earlier did not materialise. His 'power brokers' of 1985 have had a field day. Even the World Bank has withdrawn from the project, and has been forced by global public opinion to review its policy towards big dams, especially in the environmental and rehabilitation aspects.

In the case of Tehri, Indian official engineers, swore by the original safety designs and the height of the dam, till the Russians came on the scene and found it compelling to revise them. Again, there has been a total lack of sensitivity to local public opinion for the lives and interests of the local people. There is much to consider in Sunderlal Bahuguna's traditional, small-scale low-cost water harvesting systems as in Spiti, apart from the yet unresolved problems which

Indian governments, atleast, seem either incapable or unwilling to resolve the matter to the reasonable satisfaction of thousands of oustees. Bahuguna put his finger on a nub point in the quality of accountability, when he said in Tehri there was 'an environment of fear and greed,' and it is 'because the establishment has got weapons. And wherever people struggle with the establishment and its project, they will suppress the people and the rights of the people.' This has been true in scores of places; including the yet to be accounted for massacre of the Sikhs in the capital city in 1984. The gun usually supports the purse and those in power. Whatever will be the ultimate fate of Narmada and Tehri, the immediate beneficiaries have been politicians, technocrats, and contractors. 'Participation in development' has been thrown to the wolves. Delhi's thirst for water and power compels politicians and bureaucrats to push on with Tehri. The Government of India and the Delhi administration have turned the Jamuna into a sewer as far as the Chambal.

Perhaps the last commentary on this heartless lack of public accountability comes at the highest level of the heap. In 1992 Sundarlal Bahuguna was persuaded by the then Prime Minister to withdraw his fast of forty-five days with a promise of review. Again, the story of a fast of forty-nine days was enacted in 1995, with the same Prime Minister's promise of a second review. There has been no review for over three years. Public accountability should atleast have in it an element of trust from no less a person than a Prime Minister.

Let us take the sixth specific example, the denudation and firing of India's forests for the last four decades. This is a major environmental concern affecting India's soil and water conservation apart from the economic lives of millions, especially in hill and tribal areas. State governments were content to inherit and continue the colonial forest appropriating Forestry Acts, without the cooperative participation of the people. The political party and the politicians who challenged British forestry regulations in the Uttar Pradesh hills, especially in the agitations from 1917 to 1931, comfortably slipped into British shoes post-1947 and carried forest exploitation much further. The Forest department has traditionally been an 'imperium in imperio' since British days. Politicians and contractors flourished, and in these areas the major election funds came from forest contractors. Ruthless exploitation was the name of the game. The interest was more in sustainable cash, than in sustainable development.

Nor, till 1980, were official forestry minds applied to public demands for changes of systems and more 'people's participation'; and there has hardly been any progress since, because most state governments will not change old authoritarian ways. At the same time, ironically they are important to prevent further deforestation, degradation of forest lands, and deliberate firing. The only successes have been in West Bengal and Gujarat with Joint Forest Management with local people.

Again there are the same commentaries of authoritarian insensitivity (even in Van Panchayats), combined with official impotence to protect forests either against their own contractors or with alienated local people. So Indian forests have the lowest productivity among forestry nations. Chipko has been a singular and a dated protest movement. Public accountability in this field has been almost zero, despite public resentment focused by numerous NGOs.

Now for a seventh specific example, that of the Public Distribution System (PDS). Rationing in India was introduced in World War II, as in other countries. India alone continues it after half a century, ostensibly as an inflation-controlling measure, and for the weaker sections. Yet there are the same widespread complaints of irregular and inadequate supplies, plus trading in ration cards. There has been no impact of the PDS on inflation, and recently even off-take has fallen, presumably of the poorest with rising prices, defeating its objectives.

Over fifty years there has been no real public accountability for the failures of this 'socialist' system, even in the last three years since the Prime Minister announced special revamping from the ramparts of Red Fort on Independence Day. Another promise dying on political lips. Fifty years of failures in sugar controls, and one of the world's least efficient sugar businesses, has only ended in another scam in the Central government, but at least has resulted in the resignation of a cabinet minister.

In the case of the PDS, the first reason for the failure of public accountability is the weak public protest mechanisms. Second, the lack of political will, especially in excluding upper-income groups of tax assesses. Third, there has been no proper planning of demand and supply, prices and economics each year from district and town upwards.

Fourth, the failure of economists in not researching the PDS failures, besides its being neglected by the press for not being newsworthy.

Another specific example is that of the indecisiveness, spanning over twenty years, about the pollution of the Agra region, and its alleged damaging effect on the Taj Mahal. Over twenty-two years since 1973, the whole panoply of Central and state governments, executive and scientific, has failed to come to any clear conclusions about the alleged pollution from the Mathura Refinery earlier, and small-scale industries later. The main features of this sorry example of public accountability over India's most precious architectural heritage, and its earning capacity of about half the foreign tourist trade, are given below.

— Contradictions and compromises, with no clear scientific conclusions by India's top scientific echelons, including National Environment Engineering Research Institute (NEERI), replete with shocking details of lack of mutual scientific credibility.

— An apparent desire to save the Central government Mathura Refineries, and make local small-scale industries the scapegoat as late as 1993; even when the local industries of Agra region are alleged not to have grown since 1981, and the Sulphur Dioxide level in ambient air has risen from 5.64 ug/m^3 to 30 ug/m^3 currently.

— NEERI's earlier claims of 'acid rain', when the data on rain water quality showed Ph values of 6.1 to 7.7, which is a perfectly neutral range.

— There was the usual indifference on the part of the public of the Agra region in saving their most precious heritage.

— There is even a section of authoritative opinion, e.g., B.B. Lal, a scientist of the Archaeological Survey, and S.C. Pandya, a retired professor in environmental sciences and a resident of Agra, to convey, 'There is no evidence of chemical weathering and hardly any sulphation of marble, and that the Taj has hardly suffered any permanent damage.'

What an amazing commentary by the world's third largest pool of scientific and technical personnel, and its government! Where is the credibility of the highest minds in the country on matters of ascertainable scientific facts after twenty-two years, not to speak of the repeated example of the apathy of the public? Jaweed Ashraf's comments are of some significance: 'Decision-makers at all levels are behaving as if the Taj can survive if people suffer, or yet better, disappear altogether ... However, people figure very casually in the calculation of decision-makers. Politicians recognise them only at the time of elections. The executive wing is too subservient to politicians to have an independent opinion.'

As the ninth specific example, let us turn to India's public utilities, briefly and selectively, as they cover a wide field. To begin with the oldest, the Post Office, ten years and more ago, letters were delivered all over India between a day (local) and seven days. Now local mail may take nearly a week, and other mail from ten to twenty days despite increase in staff and expenditures and upgrading of communication technologies. Even international mail reaches within a week. In the same time span of ten years and more the telephones worked satisfactorily. With the advent of 'telecommunications', the functioning of Indian telephones became more problematic with higher technology — gave wrong numbers, or regaled us with recording machines telling us about engaged lines. In some places the recording machine is functional for longer hours than the dialling system. Occasionally, computerised bills are as high as the year's cost of living, and payment demands are high-handedly made before consideration of complaints. There are frequent and long failures of power systems. Public power plants have load factors as low as 20 per cent to 50 per cent; when private utilities load factors are 95 per cent to 100 per cent. India claims to have the third largest pool of technical and scientific skills. But we also have the world's largest public plundering skills with power leakages and thefts from 20 per cent to 35 per cent and inefficient water and power subsidies now cumulatively mounting to over Rs. 50,000 Cr. — with no political will to curb or control such national losses. Even in the large cities like Bombay, public utilities cannot coordinate their street-digging activities for telephones, water and power. The streets of Bombay now look like Mohenjo Daro excavations and the public can take the backseat. These fundamental public utility matters don't feature in any party's political manifesto. There is gigantic political *sauda* in public utilities, and the public can only wait for the next scandal.

When one asks why the world's third largest pool of technical and scientific skills should display such low performances, we come to the same mix of conclusions: lack of political will, in fact, political and public plundering; the absence of researched findings in the media beyond the superficial; and the absence of strong user associations at local, state, and national levels to monitor, inform, protest, and correct. Indian democracy is too submissive with the *sirkar*, a mark of a clear weakness of civic responsibility. When the limits of tolerance are reached, the public will burn public transport or attack railway offices or destroy public property; all wild-cat rebellions, but no sustained civic action. Passivity is followed by V.S. Naipal's 'million mutinies'. There is also the most critical reason for public utilities without public accountability. They are state monopolies, and there is no effective competition.

The tenth example of the lack of the public, even the legislatures' accountability, is in the gargantuan apparatus of the public-sector industrial units, state and Centre. They have been on the 'commanding heights' of the ubiquitous licence-permit Raj. Nehru and his statistical wizard, Prof. Mahalanobis reckoned PSUs would deliver profits in ten years. Again, the origins of the licence-permit raj lay in an inheritance from World War II price controls, and which was grafted on the extensive regulations of Nehru's pink socialism — a hybrid product not shared by Gandhi or Sardar Patel. Even Karl Marx did not expect socialism to emerge from a predominantly rural and feudal society, but from an industrial proletariat. Two-thirds of India's industrial proletariat of less than 30 million till the 1980s, was in the government and quasi-government sector, where they had everything to lose, including security and salaried chains. 'Autonomy' of PSUs has been a meaningless word.

Two basic questions arise concerning public accountability in this context. Why did it take forty years, the emptying of treasuries, and a near default in the payment of India's public debts in 1991, to sound the liberalisation/globalisation, deficits-controlling wake-up call? Why, during these forty years, and even five years after more competitive liberalisation/globalisation, has there been no political will for a serious re-examination and restructuring of the PSU/licence-permit heritage — apart from lowering of tariff and some delicensing — when all evidence .of the failure of most of the public sector has clearly mounted as a national liability? Is the milch cow so precious to politicians? In 1991, even the President was constrained to say, 'For far too long public funds have been looked upon as departmental dowry.'

First and foremost, the scrutiny of the Public Accounts Committees (PACs) Parliament became delayed, historical and routine. There was no fundamental questioning of policies and management systems, described as 'government by joint secretaries'. To that extent the PACs failed the nation. Few seem to know that, despite the Parliament's compulsive vote on all money bills, the huge uncontrolled internal and external borrowings are beyond the Parliament's role under Article 275(1). They can only be discussed by the Parliament, yet the Parliament's discussion, as also the role of RBI and the final control of

Finance Ministry have been sadly lacking since 1980. So India was landed with an enormous recurring interest charge, which arose from India's doubled borrowings in ten years and which brought the economy to the verge of backruptcy in 1991, without any real accountability in this fundamental of financial management. The politicians in government in the 1980s took the country for a ruinous ride, the price of which is being paid in the current decade, when India has to repay the debts of past political profligacy, without enough resources to invest in the vital infrastructure, and the basic human resource development in health and education. This has been a major lacuna in public accountability, a failure of the 'greatest' role of government, and one that has escaped public opinion.

Secondly, the reality was that whilst the Nehru legacy was political *shastra* on the surface, it proved to be a massive milch cow for decades of politicians, as with *appartchiks* in the USSR, a system which collapsed in 1989. In Mrs. Gandhi's time it became a political shibboleth to cover up the sham fight against *garibi*. Her politics was that of opportunist power, with no economic substance, a most damaging legacy of political profligacy and *sauda* eventually leading to the collapse in 1991, when India looked like a bankrupt African state.

Third, behind the Nehru heritage, there was a characteristic political and bureaucratic omniscience. Fourth, the submissiveness of the Indian public to Nehru even in the disastrous China policy. Indira Gandhi's rule, especially in the Emergency, made nonsense of public accountability. Indian citizenship became anaemic. Only after the recent realisation of the extent of political venality and plunder, has the Indian public awakened to the reality, with the beginnings of indignation of repeated unearthed scams, with the extensive criminalisation of politics, with writ petitions in the Supreme Court and High Courts, with the growth of NGOs in development and human rights. The press is kicking and free, but not investigative enough for an Indian Watergate.

The eleventh example takes us to national security. In the tradition of the Official Secrets Act — and outdated notions of security, national defence and security matters have been easily put into moth-balled wraps, with an almost total lack of public concern. Meetings of the National Security Council have been few and almost forgotten. There is no national security concept and the world knows it. The Defence Service Chiefs are invitees, not full fledged members of the Council. Parliamentary concern matches that of the Indian public, and Defence budgets are passed within minutes with hardly any informed debate or accountability. Of the 540 members of Parliament, hardly any are informed, debating members. Major issues like the future of aircraft carriers and light combat aircrafts linger for decades, with little or no informed public debate. India's position on Nuclear Proliferation Ban Treaty (NPBT) is frozen, neither signing nor testing. Even now there is hardly a government and a public appreciation, that world views on national security now rest primarily on economic and technological factors.

Together with Defence, there is the totally screened, unaccountable area of atomic energy. No less a person than

A. Gopal Krishnan, former Chairman of the Atomic Energy Regulatory Board (AERB) has revealed that :

— his study of the nuclear regulatory process was 'a total farce';

— the atomic plants of Rajasthan, Tarapur and Madras have 'specific safety deficiencies';

— old pipes carried radioactive materials, and radioactive fluids are stored in Trombay and Tarapore in tanks with welding deficiencies;

— there are consequential serious risks to the safety of employees and the surrounding populations.

Yet, no questions are raised in Parliament or the respective state legislatures, and again, no investigative journalism is done, even after Chernobyl. Going by the Indian press, one gets the impression that the only nuclear issue is the Nuclear Non-Proliferation Treaty in foreign policy. Internally, we are dangerously smug. If the AERB is subordinate to the Department of Atomic Energy, and not independent or even autonomous, how is public accountability possible? Must the public stand and wait for a disaster to happen, whilst there is continued bureaucratic and scientific cover-up?

The same mix of reasons apply more clearly and conclusively than in the previous ones. We get euphoric about the occasional war with Pakistan, and then sleep over national security for decades. Surely the armed services and nuclear matters deserve better attention from the nation, and especially its Parliament and press. The only attention given by AIR and Doordarshan are to Republic Day parades; pageant, not security!

Despite the BJP's 'sacred responsibility' and its manifestos' 'holistic approach in resource management policy and planning,' and its 'anti-pollution devices' :

— the Gujarat BJP government has been ruthless in pushing the Narmada project;

— the Shekhawat government gives active support to illegal mining of dolomite and sandstone in the Siriska Tiger Sanctuary, and is pushing the Bhilpur power plant threatening the Taj with acid rain, and spelling doom for crocodiles in the Chambal. The same government vociferously opposed the environment impact assessment notification of 1994 by HEF;

— as for pollution, Ashok Singhal (General Secretary, Vishwa Hindu Parishad) has a nephew who owns Pesticides (I) Pvt. Ltd. in Udaipur. It has been 'indiscriminatingly disposing off toxic waste and other pollutants'. Despite the Rajasthan Board's Prevention and Control of Pollution's recommendation to shift the factory, the district administration has not acted.

When it comes to cement plants, ambivalence and political opportunism appear clearest. The Congress contested the issue of three cement plants in Himachal Pradesh under the BJP. But, while in power, the Congress gave sanction for three plants, which it opposed before the election! BJP and Shiv Sena were to 'throw Enron into the sea' when out of power, when in power they renegotiated it back to land.

In West Bengal the Communist Party of India (Marxist) [CPI(M)], always 'progressive and pro-people', maintains 'a disturbing silence on the issue of industrial pollution', with Calcutta's polluting units, which the Supreme Court ordered to close on a writ petition, in 1985. It is the same with Harihar Polyfibres in Karnataka, with a Communist Industrial Trade Union (CITU)-led union. In West Bengal it is alleged that, 'Overnight land records are changed and wetlands are declared agricultural or waste lands.' This gets round environmental preservation of wetlands to enable developers to buy land legally. The Calcutta Electric Supply Corporation has been permitted to set up a 500 MVS thermal power unit on fertile agricultural land in Pujali village, in contravention of environmental guidelines.

All these are illustrative of ambivalence and political opportunism, as well as a lack of trust in the people of India by these parties who claim to represent them. Rhetoric and actions are totally inconsistent.

One may draw lessons from a recent and unique thirteenth example, public affairs in environmental matters. The special interest of this matter is that : (a) it is becoming increasingly recognised in political manifestos of the major parties; (b) it covers a wide developmental field of pollution in industry and infrastructure, and the problems of water, forests, and soil; increasingly impinging on the lives of millions of urban and rural people, including the vital 'people's participation'. In an analysis, 'Promises to keep' in *Down to Earth,* 15.5.96 the following main findings emerge in terms of political and bureaucratic behaviour and the state of public accountability.

The first and most conspicuous in all parties from BJP to CPI(M), is the widespread Indian trait of ambivalence. The greenest manifestos were those of JD, BJP and Congress. The BJP even regarded it as a 'sacred responsibility'; 'We look upon India as a holy land. Our land, air, water, our hills, forests, flora and fauna are all sacred to us.' Still influenced by the ideology of the dated Marx, the Left is least green and least touched by ecological science. The ambivalence of all, or what *Down to Earth*'s headings convey, 'A Hand in Every Pie' and 'A world of double standards,' is revealed in the remaining findings.

The second is clear and brazen political and economic opportunism by all parties. After her debut at the first International Environment Conference in Stockholm, 1972 where Indira Gandhi declared poverty was the main polluter, she and her party did little beyond developing some wildlife sanctuaries. Rajiv Gandhi's Ganga Cleaning Project of 1986, and the National Wasteland Board seemed to fizzle out in bureaucratic procedures and personal conflicts, with no political will behind them. Kamal Nath, Congress' longest-serving Environment Minister adopted a high profile at international meetings, but left the impression he was primarily interested in dollar payments by rich countries for environmental programmes; but, internally, he was in many ways no friend of the environment, or decentralised people's participation in forestry. Bhajan Lal created a furore in Parliament when, as

Rajiv Gandhi's first Environment Minister he said that the loss of lives in the case of an earthquake at the Tehri Dam had no significance for him!

The JD's Manifestos, promised a natural resource generation policy, which 'put people's survival needs at the centre, and emphasized the equity component.' It took credit for the first central notification on Joint Forest Management. But the party allowed large-scale clear felling. 'More forests were cleared in three months of JD's rule than were clear felled in a whole earlier decade.' In the JD states of Karnataka and Bihar, forestry has been neglected, and the major thrust is on the large Koel-Karno project in Bihar and Cogentrix in Karnataka. Bihar has a mega scam of embezzlement of forest funds, and no sign whatsoever in either state of decentralized, 'people survival' forestry plans. All parties share this lack of trust in the people for decentralised joint local resource management.

If, over such a wide range of examples from crime and the public distribution system to public utilities, national security and environment, there appear to be the same mix of reasons for a widespread lack of public accountability, and in both polity and society, there must be a deeper social malaise calling for analytical conclusions.

On the historical side, we have already observed that for nearly two hundred and fifty years after Aurangzeb, India lacked the experience of governing itself, which must have a significant influence on the problem. Not that we may smugly conclude that we governed ourselves well even in pre-democratic times between the death of Aurangzeb in

1707, and British Paramountcy in India in Lord Hastings' time about 1850. With the possible short-term exceptions of Tipu Sultan in the South, and Ranjit Singh in the North, the rest of India for most of the time was not well governed in this century and a half. Even under the paramount power, post-1857, the number of well-administered princely states were so few, Travancore, Cochin, Baroda, Aundh; the rest left nothing beyond personal loyalties to the rulers. (In a very unusual comparative study of the history of ideas by Hajime Nakamura, even in the ancient world, India's bent was introspective towards the *atma* as the primary aspiration; whilst ancient Greece and Japan were more practical, with the Greeks laying the foundations of scientific thinking. Even the Hindu gods share human foibles. There are no firm views on ethical social behaviour. The highest is the liberation of *atma*, and that is beyond the practical world and its phenomena.) India barely knew good, stable and widespread government for more than six of the last twenty-five centuries. Even the Chinese empire to the East, and the Turkish empire to the West, despite turbulent phases, knew longer periods of good, stable government, with systems of well-trained governing elites for long centuries down to the nineteenth century. Rajaji, that insightful statesman, once said that India had 'a governmentless civilisation.'

Small wonder then, that India in the twentieth century is weak in the fundamental social capacity of institution-building, apart from the new experience of democracy-building in the world's most pluralist society, and at a time when the social pressures of the trebling of its population in half a century is looming large. A major failure of the Congress party, in the twenty-five preparatory years before the exercise of power and in the first twenty years after Independence, was the failure to establish a good interdependent relationship of trusting, respective roles between the political and the permanent executive. The Indian rump of the ICS also shared responsibility for this in the stable and formative Nehru era. This lack of trust and understanding in mutual roles in a democratic India has had serious repercussions on the whole system of governance, affecting its stability and quality. The glib taking over of colonial control systems, without an appreciation of the roles of the political and permanent executives on the model of the cabinet system in the UK, was a mistake of the first order. Constitution-making was not enough. In a working democracy conventions are important.

When one probes deeper into the social and psycho-social side of Indian society, one comes to deeper causes for the malaise in society and government's better performances and better public accountability. Firstly, social science has shown that while Indian society has had social cooperation from the village level for religious purposes, e.g., the annual Ramlila festival, there has been hardly any social cooperation in the secular sphere, especially cutting across caste and communal boundaries. Since Rajiv Gandhi, there has hardly been any effective accountability even for the Ganga's purity. Sense of community seemed confined to family and *jati*. This lack of a tradition of secular social cooperation, and of a wider civic community has been carried into government and public affairs; as has been caste and communal divisiveness. Weak, divisive, uncivic societies make weak, divisive, uncivic governments. This does not mean to say that a superficial, 'mainstream' uniformity of the Establishment should be imposed on the world's most pluralist society. The more the Establishment has attempted to do this in the past, especially in the case of tribal India and Hindi imposition on other languages, the less national cohesion. National cohesion is far more important than official 'national integration', the Establishment's misleading slogan. Let us cohere in our different cultures; that would be true secularism. Then 900 million Indians will not only live together, but also belong and work together.

This analytical conclusion would be incomplete without a psycho-social penetration of Indian society to understand why we are what we are. Post-1991, we, the responsible intelligentia, should have the courage and intellectual integrity to face the findings of psycho-social scientists, Indian and foreign.

For good public accountability in any polity, there are some basic preconditions. First, a social consciousness of the public has to come above the private, the civic over the sectional. Second, the work ethic of result orientation, rational objectivity and impartial public accountability. This involves clear objective performance criteria of the individual and of the organisation, with fair, objective performance appraised norms; not personal or departmental fiefs run by power, whim, and personal advantage. Third, it means the autonomy and growth of responsible functionaries; not a 'culture of the *sirkar*' of dependence, hierarchical authority, and a sycophant crony culture. Ironically, the most outstanding breeders of this latter call themselves socialists, and they range from the Indira Gandhis to the Laloo Prasad Yadavs.

How far have these preconditions existed in India, pre- and post-1947? Let us seek some answers from behavioural scientists. In *Hindu Culture and Personality*, Phillip Spratt revealed a fundamental trait in our society, which he regarded as narcissistic in a Freudian sense. All societies have some narcissists, ours excel. Apart from narcissists having an undue resentment to what they perceive as criticism, hurt, or humiliation, all pointing to the difficulty of accepting objective appraisals and accountability, Spratt says, 'The caste system is the narcissist consciousness of superiority institutionalised.' And caste is a barrier to secular objective accountability. He adds, 'a nation of narcissists will show weak patriotism and public spirit,' hardly conducive to public accountability. Springing from acute narcissism, Spratt gets under the skin of the narcissist bureaucrat. 'He feels himself to be universally benevolent, endowed with omniscience and omnipotence, sitting at the controls of society, and steering the state to utopia.'

In such a psycho-social situation, performance evaluation and public accountability come hard. The preconditions for these in the public polity hardly exist, when concepts of 'public' are nonexistent or weak, and accountability is perceived as a threat to power and patronage. Rajaji referred to the tyranny of tradition and the tyranny of government, the dual tyrannies which retard objective modernisation. Two decades ago one of our rare intellectual politicians, Ashok Mehta rightly said, 'What is at stake today is not ideology but the style of functioning.' Modernisation and better public accountability call for changes in styles of functioning, changes from the feudal and bureaucratic to the modern managerial.

In his *Inner World,* Sudhir Kakar endorses 'the heightened narcissist vulnerability of the Indian male, arising from childhood rearing experience'. He says this also leads to 'an unconscious tendency to submit to an idealised omnipotent figure,' e.g., Indira Gandhi and Laloo Prasad Yadav among many others. Springing largely from parental authority and caste patterns in society, Kakar finds marked 'authority patterns and subordinate behaviour in Indian organisations'.

So when narcissism is strong, autonomy, work ethics, and self-critical faculties are weak. Omniscience and public accountability don't go together. There is an umbilical chord between dependency and state socialism, especially in authoritarian cultures. And competition only leads to psychic withdrawal and a weak, swadeshi defence mechanism.

At the end of the day, public accountability is weak or nonexistent (a) because of a traditional awe of those in power, (b) there is a low 'organizational achievement' culture for result-orientation, (c) there is low organisational objectives appraisal in the personal and kith-oriented society, and (d) there is widespread corruption and official secrecy which lead to widespread cover-up.

As a consequence of all this, Gunnar Myrdal's soft state in his *Asian Drama* continues in the Indian subcontinent;

whilst the real Asian drama is now seen in East Asia, to a lesser extent in the Gulf states, and remarkably, despite continued conflicts with Arab society, in Israel. The heart of India's problem lies here, not in the superficials of the Congress electoral claim to 'stability', or the BJP's '*Hindutva*', or the nebulous 'secular and progressive forces' of the Left. If India wishes to count as a significant power, 'styles of functioning' must change, for which cultures, values, and mind-sets also call for a change. That is in the hands of the next generation, of the future electorate, of government, media, intellectuals, and of educationalists. Politicians will remain politicians, seekers of power and opportunists, Kant's 'crooked wood' given to manipulating the state apparatus for its own ends. In a democracy, the major control mechanism has to be the politician's, balanced by the justiciary, and finally decided by the people for the polity and the economy. So there is need for a fundamental change of roles between people and politicians. The former have to be in the driving seat at and between elections through a vast plurality of institutions, official and unofficial. Control the politician, and you can control the polity. Or else that is the lesson of 'failed' and 'collapsing' African states, in which we saw at the start, marked resemblances in aspects of failure and collapse, Indian style in our case.

Some of the major specific lessons from African and Indian experience, now shared by the former USSR region, may be summed up as follows.

1. Limit the state's domain to its basic roles and its capacity to manage. That leaves the problem of the sprawling

debilitating corruption — festering public sector and license-permit raj — with little or no competition in infrastructure, and diminishing investments in both infrastructure and social development. This will be the core test of post-1996 governments in India.

2. A more limited role of the state will reduce the vast network of corruption and predatoriness, and enable higher investments and better management in security, infrastructure and social development, the core roles of the state.

3. Concentrate on better institutional performance, reducing political predatoriness and plunder, increasing public accountability; with a wider tax base and a better return to the public from public expenditures.

4. Enhancing the scope of public information, free media, decentralised civic responsibilities, better intellectual analysis of the public administration's performance and accountability. Not least, the addition of 'information' to Article 19(2)(a) of the constitution.

5. A more understanding mutual respect for each other's roles between the political and permanent executives, with better accountability to and by Parliament, legislatures and the public. It is not in the nature of power systems to make themselves publicly accountable. Accountability has to be exacted, both internally in the system, and externally by the public and its agencies, especially business organisations, NGOs and an investigative media. Basically, it means a

transition from traditional feudalism of the *'sirkari* culture' to modern management in public affairs and enterprise.

India's Security : No Leadership, No Concept

Strength respects Strength.

— Prof. Abdul Kalam

For a century and a half the British strategic concept of the security of India was intercontinental and oceanic. They were exercised by the Russian threat from the North in what they called the Great Game, culminating in the expedition to Lhasa in 1903, and they were always conscious of the security of their sea routes to India before and after the Suez Canal. In contrast, in the twenty preparatory years before Independence, despite annual superficial resolutions, the Congress party seemed oblivious to the future security of India, smug in the Vedic shell of an isolated subcontinent 'between the Northern mountains and the Southern seas'; a notion which continued post-1947 to 1962, and again post-1971. Security and survival were on the fields of the Panipats, Haldighatis, the Plasseys within India's borders. This seemed to be a cultural and civilisational view, with no larger strategic security concepts beyond, despite two thousand or more years of invasions from the North-West, and sea-power invasions from the Southern ocean in the last five hundred years. It was a narcissistic cocoon. Not even the global convulsions of World War II awakened Indians to national security concepts, as if the Japanese would have stopped at the Burma border, or Hitler in Egypt.

So, in 1947, Nehru's India made another 'tryst' with idealism in its foreign policy — which required no national security ideas to back it — not even with the harsh real-politic of the global Cold War, and the emergence of China as a strong, unified power; nor with possible future threats from Pakistan after the raiders' intrusion into Kashmir in 1948. With Non-alignment and Panchsheel, it was all glow and no guns, with a childlike disregard of Mao's famous belief of power growing from the barrel of a gun. In the memoirs of Major General A.A. Rudra, one learns of Nehru's unrealistic response to the first draft paper by the Chiefs of Staff in independent India on threats to security, asking for a government directive on defence policy. His response was: 'Rubbish, total rubbish. We don't need a defence plan. Our policy is non-violence. We foresee no military threats. Scrap the army. The police are good enough to meet our security needs.' Soon, that political judgement of India's first Prime Minister went for a six with the Pak raiders invasion of his dear Kashmir. The darling of the masses had not a clue of 'realpolitik' and India's security. What a price India has paid for political naivette since.

Let us pause to consider the serious implications of the most important political strategic document between 1947 and 1962, Sardar Patel's letter to Nehru of November 7, 1950 after the Chinese forces crossed the border into Tibet on October 7, 1950. The road to Lhasa and then to the whole northern frontier of India now lay open.

'My dear Jawaharlal,' the Sardar began, and said that he was unconvinced either by the Chinese government or the Indian ambassador and that the former 'have tried to delude us by professions of peaceful intentions' and the Chinese managed to instil into the latter 'a false sense of confidence.' He found 'a lack of firmness and unnecessary apology' of our ambassador towards the Chinese government. He significantly added, 'It is impossible to imagine any sensible person in the so-called threat to China from Anglo-American machinations in Tibet.' From Nehru and Pannikar to Krishna Menon, objective assessment seemed to be based on their personal ideological views, too trusting in the case of Communists, and too prone to distrust the West, a colonial hangover.

Note Sardar Patel's main observations, and the prescience therein for the future.

1. We have practically been 'alone in championing the cause of the Chinese entry into the UNO, and on securing assurances from the Americans on the question of Formosa (later Taiwan). Yet China continues to regard us with suspicion, scepticism, perhaps mixed with a little hostility.' The last telegram was one of 'gross discourtesy'. Then mark for the future : 'it is not a friend speaking in that language but a potential enemy'.

2. 'The Chinese interpretation of suzerainty in Tibet throws into the melting pot all frontier and commercial settlements with Tibet', which Nehru and the Foreign Office apparently took no notice of. India's buffer in Tibet, created by the British, was given up without a single protest, not to speak of hard negotiation.

3. 'Chinese irredentism and communist imperialism are different from the expansionism in and imperialism of the Western powers. The former has a cloak of ideology which makes it ten times more dangerous. In the guise of ideological expansion lie concealed racial, national and historical claims.' The Sardar saw through the Chinese in a way Nehru and others did not, the rise of the celestial empire in a new more formidable garb.

4. Patel pointed to the threat from the North and the North-East, specifically mentioning the tenuous loyalties of some people in the North-East region; adding 'they are weak spots, continuous lines of communication do not exist. There is unlimited scope for infiltration. Our outposts do not seem to be fully manned.'

5. The Sardar concluded, 'In my judgement we cannot afford to be complacent or to be vacillating'. He advocated 'enlightened firmness, strength and a clear line of policy'.

Subsequent history has proved Sardar Patel correct in every one of these prescient cautions and advice. After his tragic death in 1950, Nehru's dream world of Non-alignment, Panchsheel, Bandung, and '*Hindi-Chini Bhai*

Bhai' led India into the 'Himalayan Blunder' of 1962. The Nehru government had twelve years to heed these cautions and to prepare; more so after the Chinese occupation of Aksaichin in Ladakh in 1957. But it vacillated, it was complacent, worse, self-deluding and nation-deluding. When caught out concealing Aksaichin from the nation, Nehru brushed it aside as a place 'where not a blade of grass grows'. Is the Indian Army and Air Force wasted in the Siachen Glacier region, where too, not a blade of grass grows on icy wastes?

This was the second time Nehru's policies of straw against the Sardar's of realpolitik and substance were demonstrated. The first was in 1947-48, when the Sardar's hand drove the Pakistan raiders out of the Kashmir valley, and could have thrown them out of the whole of Kashmir when Nehru yielded to a line of occupation, and a UN plebiscite. The subsequent half century's cost of that political and military error has been incalculable.

Non-alignment, especially as staged in the UN, was wishful foreign policy of self-righteous theatre, of a colonial hang-up, a foreign policy of the traditional *pandit*'s faith in the holy Word, the *Vak*, the *Shastra*; a substitute for hard thought and decisive actions in a changing world. It was a policy of the neglect of Indian realistic security policy in diplomatic, military, and economic interests in the international field. It had no strategic security concept then and since. The inheritance of such a non-policy of words has been demonstrated in the next decades in :

— India's silent alignment, when Russian tanks invaded Hungary and Czechoslovakia; and India's silent acquiescence when later Russia invaded Afghanistan, leading to a long destabilisation of India's North-West approaches;

— India's essential isolation in the international community, even in Asia;

— its lack of dividends in supporting a mythical Pan-Arabism over Israel even after several oil crises, in which India got none of the badly needed oil concessions;

— its recent isolation in the Nuclear Non-Prolification Treaty (NNPT) affair and the dismal lack of support for a Security Council seat. Non-alignment has proved to be a useless dodo. K. Shankar Bajpai has said in 'Pursuit of national Interest', 'Today it is a totally outdated supposition that there is a social body of common interest called non-alignment, on whose shoulders we could ride high, that stifles objective thinking and lands us in these embarrassments' (*The Hindustan Times* 2.11.96). Strangely, Indian politicians are totally engrossed in power politics in India. In foreign affairs they cannot overcome 'an aversion to power politics' in Bajpai's words. We tend to treat international issues as a kind of Ramlila, in which Ram has to assume self-righteous postures — Panchsheel to NNPT for the benefit of mankind. '*Dikhane ke liye*', as H.N. Bahuguna revealed in a transparent moment. Nothing is more facile and dangerous than a single idea like 'Non-alignment', when we have none other in changing international power equations.

When the crunch came in 1962 after all the Non-aligned theatre in Bandung, Delhi, and the UN, India was unprepared, its troops committed to high altitude warfare without acclimatisation, proper clothing and equipment, bad generalship, and a humiliating defeat. Just prior to the Chinese push South, after an initial incursion, Nehru flew off to Sri Lanka with a grand command to 'throw them out' without a strategic concept of any kind, as if it were a mere police action. The government even forgot that it had an Air Force, which could have been used with deterrent effect in the North East Frontier Agency (NEFA) border, where the Chinese had collected 20,000 troops for the thrust South since Patel's clear warnings.

For most of these twelve years, India's security virtually lay in the theoretical ideological minds of only two persons, Nehru and Krishna Menon. This was a fatal flaw. It is said that Nehru, crest-fallen after 1962 and hurt by Chinese deceit, virtually died of a broken heart. India died of shame, all its tall diplomatic pretensions as a leader of the Non-aligned movement, such unction to ideological Indian souls, shattered. The General Henderson-Brooks military report on NEFA lies buried and forgotten in a non-transparent government. In shame, it seems as if the Parliament and the people of India do not want to reveal and learn from it, a bad dream of Nehru's empty foreign policy. The Sardar's wise, pragmatic, and specific policy advice seemed to have been forgotten in the nation's unctuous, self-deluding love-affair with Nehru and his policies of words, then and since, with no defence strategy and a foreign policy leading to isolation.

In 'War in the High Himalaya', General D.K. Palit revealed that Indian political, military and civil bureaucratic leadership were totally unprepared to formulate and implement a coherent national security policy. The armed forces were not integrated with the government. There was no systematic process of intelligence assessments.

There was no attempt to assess the strength of the Chinese forces in Tibet. The Prime Minister, the government and the ruling party were responsible for this. None of these deficiencies have since been rectified. Security and intelligence assessments have been 'adhocist and personality oriented', according to K. Subramanyam, Director, Institute of Defence Studies and Analysis. The security malaise is a lingering weakness of what passes for Indian political leadership.

Having learnt the security lessons of NEFA, 1962, let us now turn to the lessons learnt from Bangladesh, 1971, and Sri Lanka, 1987.

In early 1971 Mrs. Gandhi had made up her mind to take action about Bangladesh. When she conveyed this to General S. Manekshaw, then Chief of Army Staff, he cautioned her in straight soldierly language. Immediate, precipitate action involved defeat. (You can't get armies to win wars by pressing political buttons, as our politicians seem to think, if you neglect security strategy earlier). 'Not till I am ready, Madam,' was General Manekshaw's professional response. She had no sensible option. When Manekshaw was ready by December, he struck in India's most decisive military operation in these fifty years, and it was over in sixteen days, a twin, well-coordinated military and political blow to Pakistan, after the indecisive war of 1965-66. Another important lesson in terms of economic sinews of security was the fact that the Green Revolution made the US gesture of an aircraft carrier in the Bay of Bengal innocuous. Had India still been dependent on PL 480 foodgrains, Bangladesh may not have happened. Proof that economic sinews and political and military strategies have to go together in a world where power is shifting to the economic realm.

This lesson was lost by Rajiv Gandhi's time. The then Chief of Staff did not have the prudence or the guts to tell him, 'Not till I am ready, Sir'. So we plunged in mindlessly without intelligence, without a proper appreciation of the Liberation Tigers of Tamil Eelam, which India is alleged to have trained earlier, and with confused political objectives between loyalty to Tamils at home, and playing to President Jayawardhane's interests in Sri Lanka. The results were disastrous, a wounding drain over a year and a half, a thousand casualities, and a virtual withdrawal, with the next President of Sri Lanka telling India to get out. *Jagatguru* flexed his unprepared limbs, and an impetuous mind brought a result quite contrary to Bangladesh, 1971. Was there any security strategy in the Sri Lankan episode? When the holy *Jagatguru* posture of grandfather Nehru turned into the psychology of a preponderant regional power in grandson, Rajiv; the Indian Peace Keeping Force should never have been exposed to such an unpopular and embarrassing situation, and in the face of the adverse opinions in SAARC and the world outside. It was symptomatic of political, diplomatic, and military bankruptcy in the absense of clear, long-term strategic concepts. To justify himself, Rajiv Gandhi need not have reinvented his mother's 'foreign hand', in saying the Sri Lanka adventure was to save Trincomalee and Sri Lanka from a foreign power. The Lankan adventure was a piece of gross political and military mismanagement under an amateur Prime Minister, and a military establishment made subservient by his mother and grandfather. One of the most serious of the Nehru dynasty's legacies is this total lack of institutionalised security management, and a realistic foreign and military strategy.

In the absence of that crucial concept Mrs. Gandhi indulged in nuclear Pokharan posturing earlier, a one-person strategic decision, reminiscent of the two-person foreign policy of Nehru and Krishna Menon. For twenty years thereafter, in the absence of a long-term security strategy, we 'kept our options open'; neither taking the opportunity to make more nuclear explosions to clearly establish India as a nuclear power with a few nuclear weapons, nor signing NNPT. Again, posturing as *Jagatguru* for total nuclear disarmament, was like acting like Asoka after the Kalinga War in an ancient world; then in a purely internal, not an international context. Even with *ahimsa* on his rock edicts, there is no historical evidence of Asoka totally disarming. Keeping his options open with a concealed mace, *Jagatguru* was confused and totally isolated once again in the world community of nations. As Prof. Abdul Kalam, father of the missile programme has said, 'strength respects strength'. While we may all deplore nuclear weapons, no state has become a member of the Pugwash Club. Optionless pious posturing in the face of China's nuclear missiles in Tibet aimed South, and Pakistan frantically going nuclear, is plain hogwash in the real world of power and security. More so, when Mrs. Gandhi knew that her 1967 mission with Dr. Vikram Sarabhai, Chairman, Atomic Energy Commission and her Secretary, L.K. Jha, to seek guarantees from Russia, France, Britain and US proved fruitless. The Pokharan posture was no security protection.

For forty years Indian foreign policy suffered from five lingering illusions. First, the illusion of the USSR as a durable support in international affairs, especially in armaments. To that extent, India has been dependent to the extent of over 70 per cent for arms supplies from one source only, a source disrupted in the last eight years, and, to that extent, a reflection on India's diplomatic isolation. The second was an illusion of Non-alignment and Pan Arabism as a political force, and a self-denial of the benefits of diplomatic, economic and military links with Israel and the West. This was also reminiscent of its scared attitude of having no links with Taiwan, an Asian economic power in its own right. Western governments knew that most of the Non-aligned shared no more than a wordy platform. When the chips were down, they knew which side of their bread was buttered and voted accordingly in the UN. The third illusion was the irrelevance of East Asia, another isolation from the most dynamic part of Asia, and the future high potential of the Asian-Pacific region, especially its exclusion from ASEAN. The fourth illusion was that India could be self-sufficient and self-reliant with the wrong *swadeshi* ideas, with only 0.5 per cent of the world's trade; fondly imagining most of these decades that the world's investors would beat a path to the Gateway of India, if only India raises a welcoming finger. A foreign policy and the economic policies based on such facile assumptions only reflected ignorance of global economic realities, and that smugness in a narcissistic cocoon. In it, how convenient it was for Mrs. Gandhi and others to invent 'the foreign hand', when internal matters went beyond their competence! The fifth illusion was that India remained an absolute sovereign state when international technology, finance, and communications had bypassed sovereign states in the international movements of technology, money, and communications; and with these techno-economic power too was eroded. All five add up to self-induced isolation and impotence. I may call these five illusions Panchmaya, in contrast to the once-glib Panchsheel. The Panchsheel may have been long forgotten, but the Panchmaya has haunted our decision-making processes these fifty years. India's leaders have been afraid to step out into the world on hard ground, beyond speechifying platforms and look-good postures.

India's internal insecurity has seen V.S. Naipaul's 'million mutinees', as a result of weak government and short-sighted politics. In 1950, Sardar Patel had pointed to the alienation of the North-East. Nehru showed empathy with the North-East tribes. Since then, the North-East has been a hot-bed of tribal unrest, with no signs of resolution in the last thirty years. The unrest in Kashmir is, partly, a legacy of Nehru's naive unfinished business after the tribal raiders in 1947-48; and partly subsequent misgovernment and rigging of elections, which seriously alienated the Kashmiri people, and gave Pakistan a cause for post-partition, and post-Bangladesh revenge. Similarly, the Punjab since Bhindranwala, initially a creation of the ruling Congress, was another case of unsecular politics, with Mrs. Gandhi playing the Hindu card, and a tragic alienation of the Sikhs, one of India's proudest and most valuable communities. The calamity of Amritsar was avoidable earlier, and with better intelligence; unless, as is suspected, Mrs. Gandhi herself wanted a showdown for her own political ends. The Delhi massacre of Sikhs, the Ayodhya temple destruction, showed the pusillanimity of the Central government, if not its connivance in some measure — both inexcusable. Extremist groups in North Bengal, Assam, Bihar and Andhra have caused the states to 'wither away' in many regions over prolonged periods of time, with private police of landlords and ideological extremist cadres filling the state's vacuum. Even Bodh Gaya, a hallowed centre of international Buddhist pilgrimage, cannot be protected from lawlessness and attacks on pilgrims. Insurgency and terrorism have been a continuing feature. There has been a thin line dividing political parties, even ruling ones and the mafia; apart from politicians of all parties not having the guts to govern and give citizens the basic law and order.

All this is happening despite the growth of several police forces from a strength of 95,000 in 1947 to 1.2 million, of whom 3.25 lakh comprise the armed element. The new armed police forces of the union since the Sixties, referred to as the Central Para Military Forces, and the army are called upon by the states to do all manner of jobs, in natural calamities, in communal riots, in elections, in anti-terrorist activities, and now in the capital, Delhi in anti-Dengue operations! It shows the near complete failure of state governments in civil administration. Incompetent, weak politicians, the straw of the polity, constantly fall back on the paramilitary and army, to the detriment of their training and functions in the areas for which they were meant. These are totally spineless governments, whose primary objective has been power and plunder, not good government. This is a fundamental challenge to Indian democracy, to make the governors govern, and stop looting.

Mr. N.N. Vohra, IAS and former Home Secretary, has pointed to the politicisation of the police, and the steady deprivation of powers of the Home Ministry by the Cabinet Secretariat under the Prime Minister. It no longer manages the IAS cadre or controls the functioning of CBI. Both the external intelligence agency and the Joint Intelligence Committee are under the Cabinet Secretariat under the Prime Minister. Finance has charge of economic administration in Customs, Excise, Enforcement Directorate, Narcotics, Coast guard, and air ports function under the Civil Aviation Ministry. He writes 'The grave hazard of the Home Ministry continuing to manage internal security through 'coordination' (which he did not add is no forte of Indian government), was amply demonstrated in December, 1995, when a foreign aircraft paradropped arms and ammunition in Purulia and made several unauthorised landings on Indian airports. The investigations so far have not been able to identify for whom the lethal cargo was meant!'

All these fractured, uncoordinated responsibilities for India's security, despite some apparent centralisation in Cabinet Secretariat and the Prime Minister's Office, is in the face of the complex inter-connectivity between the underworld (Indian and foreign), organised crime, narcotics flow, terrorism, insurgency, and some unreliable politicians. K Subramanyam says, 'The politician-bureaucrat organised crime has a vested interest in ensuring that such coordinated national security management is not set up.' His conclusion is disastrous. 'Successive political leaderships do not appear to have realised the need for institutional arrangements to safeguard the security of the Republic. They have been content to deal with the highly complex task in an adhocist and personalized style. National security has not been on the top of their agenda ... The Republic is more vulnerable today than ever before and its ability to tackle the security challenges is diminishing with each passing day.' (*India International Centre Quarterly,* Spring, 1996). Perhaps it may be ironical to mention an observation by V.N. Narayan in 'Intolerant Society, Insecure State': 'Meanwhile P.V. Narasimha Rao is on his way to Vidhan Bhavan in his bullet proof limousine accompanied by a convoy of commando-filled cars to face charges of cheating, forgery and bribery. What a state of security to be in.' (Perspective, *The Hindustan Times*, 20.10.96)

I would only add that : (a) right from Nehru's time Indian political leadership has been totally uneducated in national and international security matters, not even appreciating or understanding the importance of politico-military strategic concepts and planning; and (b) later, post-1971, they have been so absorbed in their own political survival, as to have neither time nor inclination for India's security needs. Hence, it is virtually not on their agenda. Nothing more scathing can be said for these men and women of straw in the near-total neglect of the nation's primary function in government.

So we come to the recent past in 1990-91, when the treasuries of India were empty, when India was on the verge of default on its foreign debt payments, when all past policies which had brought India to this terminal condition had failed after forty years of planned development. We also come to the problems of the present and the future. Apart from the economic mismanagement referred to in the previous chapters, which inevitably weakened India's strength and security, it would be desirable to fall back on the state of India's armaments in all three services, and the writings of three retired military officers, to warn us of the dangers ahead.

India's war machine is aging and shrinking; it is not being replaced with up-to-date technology. It is in an armaments technology/payments trap because of political neglect, especially in the last decade. Inadequate resources are passed in the annual Defence budget in eight minutes to six hours, a damaging indication of even Parliament's neglect of matters of national security. The few revealed scams amount to about Rs. 10,000 Cr. of political-bureaucratic loot, but the largest security arm of the nation, the army can barely be spared an extra Rs. 2,000 Cr. in the budget.

What has happened to the Defence Research and Development Organisation (DRDO), with forty highly sophisticated laboratories, twelve PSUs in production, and forty-two Ordnance factories, besides large specific outfits for indigenous projects like the Arjuna tank? In 1989, of the 989 ongoing projects, 618 were dropped. The reasons given were non-completion and non-availability of funds. There is no mention of years of probable mismanagement. Why were 989 projects taken up for India's defence needs, if two-thirds of them had to be dropped? Does government not ensure the requisite ongoing funds beyond the year's budget? Why is no one accountable? Another 'systems failure'? Even the gods cannot tell us. There is no transparency and no public debate or accountability.

The Indian Army needs a hundred new tanks a year to replace the old ones. It has been getting far fewer; in 1995-96 it got only fifteen. The army's tank regiments have shrunk. The artillery asked for six hundred-odd 155 mm self-propelled guns since the end of the 1980s. They are high priority as Pakistan has had US M109-A2 for years. The army had to settle for a gun fitted on T-72 tank chassis, sacrificing a tactical battlefield advantage. The army was also hopeful of acquiring the 150 km Prithvi, but the funds caused problems again.

The Navy is likely to be left with no aircraft carrier till 2005. Its allocation in the 1995-96 budget of Rs. 1,286 Cr. would suffice for only two submarines. Three-fourths of the Navy's ships are due for refitting. The Navy will have twenty-six ships against thirty-six earlier, a shrunk force with oceanic responsibilities. But our politicians have pre-Vasco de Gama minds.

The worst hit seems to be the Air Force, the most critical long-range strike arm. For ages its demand for an advanced jet trainer has been pending, while pilots have to go straight on to MIGs and Jaguars, with consequential high accident rates. As many as eighty-nine aircrafts have been lost. A case of being penny wise and pound foolish. There has been no modernisation of the air fleet for a decade, calling for upgrading and extensions of old aircraft. The latest order for twenty-five to thirty MIG 29s came through only because the Russians offered credit! While the government is dragging its feet on Sukhoi-30 purchases, Pakistan is shopping for Mirage-2000s and Sukhoi-27s.

The break-up of the USSR coincided with India's resource crunch, and all these years Indian governments have ignored the potential of the Indian private sector, which should have been brought into military technology with the PSUs and ordnance factories thirty years ago; but there was the Nehru-Krishna Menon ideological bias, also carried into later years. In all advanced Western countries, it is the private sector which has produced arms, ships, and aircraft. In the last ten years the Indian government has — just drifted. Parliament has been oblivious. Thanks to Mr. Narasimha Rao, it has voted its members over Rs. 1,000 Cr. a year for constituency development! If one computes this amount for a single five-year term, and adds Rs. 10,000 Cr. of political scams, the Indian Army could have bought a hundred and fifty tanks with this amount at

1995-96 prices, against the budget money for only fifteen! Mr. Rao's security of tenure came before the nation's security.

In an article, 'Defense Expenditure and Foreign policy', Brigadier N.B. Grant goes to the fundamental fact that it is foreign policy that should determine the Defence Services security preparations, its training, its perceptions of threats, and its expenditures. Far from doing this, Indian foreign policy is virtually delinked from defence preparedness. He goes on to say that a foreign policy of Non-alignment implies isolation against threats, no allies, and a com-pulsion to maintain a permanent force to defend 8,000 kms. of national borders on land and sea. One wonders whether Parliament and government have ever considered the cost implications of this. Brigadier Grant rightly asks, 'Can we afford to continue to base our national security on the policy of non-aligned defence?' The running down of the war machine in the last decade shows that it is obviously not so. So what new foreign, diplomatic, economic, and military policies, are called for? Even that question cannot be answered.

India's entire security policy needs serious review in the light of the following significant deficiencies :

— in the absence of a regular National Security Council, of which the three Service Chiefs should be full time members;

— when there is a gap in communication between the Prime Minister and the Service Chiefs; (Mr. P.V. Narasimha Rao probably saw them on ceremonial occasions like Republic Day);

— when there is no system whereby the Defence Minister liases with the Foreign Minister, and can get a periodic exchange of views on major security threats and likely future developments;

— when the Defence Minister has no system even within his own ministry to get an analytical and unbiased appreciation of the budget needs and allotments to each of the services;

— when there is no Joint Chief of Staff of the three services to coordinate defence strategies in the light of perceived threats;

— when our disjointed Intelligence Services can be so unreliable as they were in the Sri Lanka adventure;

— and, lastly when foreign and economic policies are virtually divorced, and only reactive.

All these add up to a total lack of a national strategic mind in government, apart from the absence of informed parliamentary interest and debate.

General A.M. Vohra, a former Army Commander, and General P.M. Kathpalia, former Director-General, Military Intelligence, confirm, 'There is little coordination in peace and no integration of operational plans. The degree of cooperation depends purely on the personalities of the three chiefs. Politicians have not heeded the need for fool-proof inter-services coordination. In 1947 India started with the ideal of a Chief of Defence Staff, the Army Chief being designated Commander-in-Chief of the three services. It is said politicians began to have reservations on this because he would be too strong, and they feared 'a coup'.' If anything, Mrs. Gandhi perpetrated a coup in the mid-Seventies with the Emergency. Later, politicians have been parties to recurring local coups of the armed mafia when the politicised police have been rendered ineffective. General Vohra believed that if there had been a Chief of Defence staff, Operation Blue Star, Exercise Brass Tacks, and the deteriorating situation in Jammu and Kashmir would have received coordinated, multi-dimensional consideration and integrated plans to meet the crises, instead of one ministry's analysis and plans. General Kathpalia was of the view that 'the tremendous value of combined operations is not fully appreciated'. He believed that combined coordination should not be confined to the three services, but should extend to the paramilitary forces also. 'Imagine the strategic advantage one shall have', he added, 'when India has an amphibious capability to launch divisional groups forces under an air umbrella.' They re-emphasised the need for the national Security Council, for 'to safeguard national interest needs an inter-ministerial body'. (*The Economic Times*, 1.8.90.) The interdependence of all the armed forces today, and their organisation and preparation for joint operations to project power in crises in relevant places is a *sine qua non* of military thinking in the contemporary world.

Why are these things not happening in India? Why is India's war machine running down when the arms race is now spreading to the Middle East and East Asia? Why is there no coordination between foreign and security policies, between the three different Defence Services? Why is there no coordination between India's security, foreign relations, and economic policies? Why does India's security, the first priority, not have enough resources, nor adequate attention of political minds in government and Parliament; when India's isolation has been so apparent and when all land and sea frontiers are vulnerable, when India's old Achilles' heel, the North-West is more vulnerable than ever since Babar, with the accumulating forces of state and non-state Islamic fundamentalism, when Chinese moves appear to point to an encirclement of India from the Karakoram Highway, to Tibet, Burma, and the Indian ocean? Indian politicians seem to be blind and deaf to all this. Even the NEFA disaster and the Sri Lankan misadventure, apart from the slow bleeding of terrorist warfare in Kashmir has not taught politicians, Parliament and the intelligentia a serious lesson.

Why? The question demands clear, open, penetrating answers if India is to be safe in the future.

I would put the first reason in past Indian 'thought ways' in Indian security, a concept in Ken Booth's 'Strategy and Ethnocentrism'. As I have mentioned earlier, it goes back to the smug notion of the Vedic shell between 'northern mountains and southern seas', reinforced by ethnocentrism and a narcissist cocoon. India has not acquired geo-political thinking, since Nehru. Its political leaders from Nehru to Narsimha Rao have had no education in geopolitical affairs and straegic military thinking; nor did they want to learn. Theirs was a Brahmanical Omniscience of the *Jagatguru*. Except when attacked in 1948, 1965-66, and self-induced in

1971 in Bangladesh, and in 1987 in Sri Lanka, national security is taken for granted by all. Unlike leaders in America, Europe, Russia, China and Vietnam, as young men they never served in the Defence Services. Their minds could barely transcend police actions. They have shown poor statecraft in a 'soft state', in which their primary concerns have been either to cut a fine figure in words on public and foreign platforms; or be almost totally engrossed in their own survival, power, patronage and loot in a country of 'a million mutinies'. Indians tend to be ad hoc and personal. A holistic grand strategy on land, sea, air and space in their own continent Asia is not for them. The lessons of Desert Storm blew over like a passing monsoon, leaving only a marginal concern for crude oil. Then a bankrupt government swallowed Rs. 8,000 Cr. from the Oil Pool Account, as if that account had no earlier purpose. In a year the deficit of the oil pool is likely to rise to Rs. 15,500 Cr. Oil, a basic sinew of war and peace, is a major threatened resource, with oil companies being paid just half the international price, underpricing, as in the whole infrastructure, and our incapacity to invest more in indigenous oil development. India is heading for a third oil crisis; this one is self-inflicted by mindless men of straw who, in their weakly administered underpricing policy, have created a future oil threat to the nation's security in a basic resource for the economy and the defence machine.

In short, Indian political leaders of straw have been bankrupt in strategic minds and in the public purse. India's biggest weakness is in its political leadership. And that is a fatal flaw of the Indian state, which not Brahma, but only the public of India can correct; and only if it rises above its so-called leaders. This is the basic lesson of these fifty years. Would that our military top brass were less subservient to a civil power ignorant of security strategy! We need more combinations of Manekshaw and Seshan in uniform. Even the retired can give voice to India's security needs more strongly.

The day of reckoning must come. Asia is both on the move and on the boil. China is seen, even in America, as the rising global power of the next twenty years. The future of Pakistan and Afghanistan is in a fire of uncertainty, and so will Central Asia be beyond their frontiers. Myanmar is a future question mark. So many powers have major stakes in the Indian ocean, at least as long as Arab oil lasts. Where are India's future coherent geopolitical-cum-international trade policies and strategies? In what shape are the sinews of India's strengths, its armed services, its infrastructure, its technologies, its balance of payments, its internal resources, its very self-confidence?

Agenda for the Future : Main Questions

Experience is a good teacher, but she sends in terrific bills.

– Mina Antrim,
Naked Truth and Veiled Illusions

Behind the 'naked truth and the veiled illusions' of the last fifty years since Independence, and for the sake of concluding clarity, could we put on the table of the next generation the main inherited questions from the past for a new nation of over a billion human beings, the second largest on earth after China, still with the largest numbers of illiterate and poor? In Gandhi's words, India is still a nation 'that walks on one leg', as women are still not literate and empowered; forget the political tricks of superficial 'reservations'. Apart from the lessons of the last fifty years, there is the lacuna of two hundred and fifty years between Aurangzeb and Mountbatten, when India lost the precious experience of managing its own affairs, unlike most Asians from Japan to Turkey. Will the leaders of the future be good learners from the teachers of the past? If not, those 'terrific bills' of the past. will mount horrifically in the future. The leaders of the past, especially those of the past thirty years, have done their worst, and they now await the dustbin of history.

First, how can we work as a democratic nation rising from poverty, insecurity, and corrupt misgovernment, and recognise that, after the now wind-swept umbrella party of the post-Independence Congress, there are no majorities? After the passing of that 'veiled illusion' of unity under one All-India ruling party, we have to recognise the hard historical reality that India comprises groups of minorities in the world's most pluralist country. The naked truths are just dawning through recent elections and the fading out of the Congress :

— that the Hindu majority of 80 per cent is a political myth ironically created by the Muslim League, pre-partition, and now being resurrected by the *Hindutva parivar* quite unrelated to practical politics;

— that the Hindus have never in all history, and since 1947, ever acted as a coherent political community with their caste, linguistic, and power divisions;

— that the voting pattern cuts across all faiths, castes, linguistic groups, and also across those who label themselves as secular, Left and Right; and this cross voting will increase as Indian democracy evolves into new coalitions of minority interests in a large federal state, and with increasing inter-marriages in a growing middle class.

How can we find pragmatic, mutual grounds for coalescence, if in reality we are all minorities, putting national issues commanding a wider electorate, above the sectional ones of caste, religion, or language with smaller, divisive electorates, which end up with hung legislatures and no stable democratic governments? The Deve Gowda United Front government with a Common Minimum Programme (CMP) at the Centre was the first significant signal of the need for the future coalescence of minorities as a political compulsion, if India is to be held together. It must be noted that even that CMP :

— makes no mention of national security policies in External and Defence affairs;

— nor does it mention anything about international competitiveness with higher productivity and better technologies in global trade; only the old atavistic and failed mind-frames of 'protecting interests of agriculture, industry and genetic resources by forging international and multilateral agreements', as if reliance on such inter-governmental agreements in the past have not reduced India to a 0.5 per cent economy in international trade;

— there is no mention of a viable and strong infrastructure to provide the sinews for economic and military security, only a pathetic 'attracting long-term and foreign funding', since partly vitiated;

— nor is there any important mention of social development in health and education, despite India's shameful ranking among the lowest in the international HDI; only the dubious disinvestment proceeds of PSUs — with no mention of making them viable — to go to health, education, and new public investment projects! A case of short-term amnesia when, in the previous year, against a planned PSU disinvestment of Rs. 7,000 Cr., the Indian market bought less than Rs. 150 Cr.

Does it make sense for a foreign policy to aim at a Security Council seat, and remain at the bottom rung of the international HDI? Is this what CMP amounts to in the end?

So, secondly, how can a strong public demand be created for the above basic and holistic aspects for India's future security strategy, internal and external, a strategy grounded on geo-political basis, at least in the Asian-Pacific region, together with the long neglect of infrastructures and the HDI? This should include the political (realpolitik in Defence, Foreign, and international trade policies), the economic (financial discipline of Indian governments and the 20 million or so privileged employees in them, bloating the nation's taxes and borrowings at the cost of over 900 million of the rest, especially the 350 million in the lowest human development area), the technological (the indispensible new sinews of modern life and security in peace and war), and the military capacity of projecting combined operation power on land, sea, and in the air in areas of India's vital interests. 'Only strength respects strength.'

Any political party which can put these holistic and strategic concerns into an imaginative core strategy for India's future — with security, good government, and growth out of poverty as its three main platforms — is likely to be a future winner, transcending the smaller electorates of caste, faith, and language. The latter, Masjid, Mandir and Mandal have ended up with hung legislatures, no stable democratic government, and no stable base for even the stability of power of politicians. Exploitative men and women of straw and cardboard, with no larger vision for the electorate, have played their zero-sum games for thirty years to their own powerless end, and that of the nation. They have nothing to show for it, except the proceeds of massive loot with the widespread misuse of power; leaving India with a shameful 0.5 per cent of world trade, and an even more shameful low place in the HDI.

Those who seek power as leaders of coalescing minority groups should also remember the reality that 75 per cent of the purchasing power of India comes from about 65 per cent of the nation in the age groups twelve to forty-five. Tomorrow they will determine the voting power, over half of them concentrated in urban India, and cutting across sectional segments of faith, caste, and language. They will be hard-headed about a better quality of life, higher purchasing power with low inflation, widening market choices with competition, more efficient infrastructures, less *'dikhane ke liye'* politics, and far less corruption. They will want good, stable governments, with men and women of substance as leaders. Past *leaderi* of atavistic, backward states and regions should also remember their most enterprising and able people will migrate, either abroad or to more developed states and regions in India. They will have no power to prevent this. They will be left with the dregs at the bottom of the HDI, and social and political systems which cannot attract capital investments, Indian or foreign. It may be marked that the highest concentrations of human development and infrastructure in the country also attract the highest investments. They are Delhi, Bombay, Bangalore and Gujarat. Maharashtra and West Bengal have paid 'terrific bills' as their past experience has not been a good teacher, and they have been poor and belated learners. That applies, in a most pronounced fashion, to the whole of the Hindi belt. Haryana is benefitting from a neighbourhood over-spill from Delhi.

Third, how can the Parliament and the Judiciary be made more effective and speedier arbiters of competing interests of a nation of minorities, political, economic and social interests; with more transparency and more public accountability of the Executive before the Constitution and the law? Parliamentary Committees need better political and executive leadership, supported by research, as in Western democratic legislatures. Parliament and its Committees need to set an example to the nation in hard work and high productivity, and not be a spectacle of unproductive *tamasha*. Parliament will only be sovereign when it gets good public accountability for better results from the Executive. Or else it will only be a sovereign conniver of all the misuse of power and resources of the Executive, which the nation has witnessed in the past. Hence the 'terrific bills' of a nation sinking deeper into insecurity, indebtedness, corruption, and unbeaten human degradation; summed up in all its aspects in poverty and that low HDI, of which we hear nothing from Parliament or the Planning Commission, whose central task this is. A democracy without an empowered people, and a Parliament and legislatures which yet cannot empower themselves, is no democracy.

Let those political culprits who have recently complained of 'judicial activism' when caught out and made more accountable, remember it is the product of a more active citizenship in a democracy of which they are supposed to be trustees. The reality is not too much 'judicial activism', (far too little in the past in fact), but far too much abuse of power by politicians and officials with widespread 'systems failures' (or bad government) and private loot by public authorities. If 'judicial activism' can bring better accountability and curb widespread abuse of power, the people of India want more of it, not less. The electorate will not be dumb, driven cattle as before. The new electorate will demand new politicians and new 'quality of life' politics.

Fourth, how to make a sustainable, growing economy, and sustainable natural resources of land, water, forests meet the needs of populations exceeding one billion? How can the sustainable resources of land, water and forests be managed for this huge population? How can pragmatic links — sensible trade-offs — be built between economic development and sustainable environmental development? The choice does not lie with only one of the politicians. It is a complex problem calling for political and professional know-how and imagination of a high order, beyond narrow claims on river waters. It will require new networking cadres of professionals who can visualise and plan beyond nineteenth-century departments — cities and hinterlands, natural agro-climatic zones, river catchments and sub-catchments as overall fields of sustainable life and planning. It will need the restructuring of minds, institutions, systems, the reconceptualising of planning of inter-dependencies, the redesigning of governments. Politicians and bureaucrats should appreciate that the combining of eco-systems in environment and economics in human development compels going down realistically to the grass roots of sub-catchments, natural resources, and local people in town and country for the most basic needs of clean water, good soil, fuel and fodder sustainable crop productivity, cleaner air, cleaner infrastructures, and a better quality of life. Poor eco-systems mean poor people, despite government expenditures. No anti-poverty programmes can succeed by mere expenditures if soils deteriorate, if water sources are depleted and fouled, if polluted water and air make people sick, if decimated forests and eroded soils can no longer absorb moisture. Down that road lies poverty, famine, disease, unemployment, and depleted natural resources, which the mints of government cannot restore. Decentralised expenditures by themselves are only decentralised opportunities for more loot. They must go with these basic eco-development projects which are employment-intensive, women-oriented, and the natural resource foundation for rural prosperity.

Fifthly, if the basis of modern civilisation and national economic growth and national security is energy, one of the most neglected of questions is a National Energy Policy for all classes, and for the basic sinews of infrastructure, industry, and agriculture. The Nehruvian model and mind-frame have got us into a quagmire of unsustainable administered oil pricing — usually politically shelved — into a practice of robbing Peter (oil companies and the Oil Price Pool) by Paul (the Finance ministry), leading to the same 'no money anywhere' situation, as in power and water mismanagement. Then there is the hard reality of no further significant oilfields after Bombay High. Finally, the absence of competitive efficiencies in energy usage from oil companies and SEBs to motor vehicles and irrigation pumps.

So, how can our energy problems be overcome?

For the rural poor, the 70 per cent living on non-conventional energy, there seem to be no option to a national bio-mass programme in village common lands, wastelands, and national forests to raise productivity of firewood, fodder, bagasse, and make widespread and viable mini-hydel, *gobar* gas, LPG gas, solar drying and cooking. This needs a Sam Pitroda-type mission, initiated by the Centre, but implemented by the states. Another important Planning Commission task among many that 'went wrong' in Mr. Deve Gowda's question.

Next, if the future lies with natural gas, where are the twenty-year programmes for it? Pipelines for natural gas from Oman and Central Asia, occasionally featured by the press, appear to be pipe dreams in terms of political, technological and economic feasibility. Where, then, are realistic plans for natural gas? What of the future of coal? And of the hopeful transition from carbon to hydrogen, a twenty-first century prospect? Bogged down in the past nuclear dilemma, India has not begun to think seriously of the transition to hydrogen, in our static mind-sets.

In the organised sector, there appears to be another no-option alternative, the abolition of unsustainable and distorted administered prices. Let prices be determined by competitive markets. Government and political parties would be free from the fears of rising prices and rising subsidies, the twin jinx.

The third problem of gross inefficiencies of energy again can only be cured by more market competition in pricing, and fuel efficiencies by the automobile industry. Maruti has led the way. More competition will improve fuel efficiencies as an important competitive edge in future. The Planning Commission — a centrepiece of 'What went wrong?' — seems to have ignored the lesson of Western countries after the oil crisis of 1973, when the ratio of energy inputs to economic growth was brought down to 0.7:1. In India it is still over 1:1, another vital hidden inefficiency in that failed model.

India now needs a market-oriented K.D. Malaviya, in the changed energy scenario, in which past policies are unsustainable, politically and economically. But this too requires leaders of substance with political will, not straw.

How can the state, with less demanding roles than that expected in the Nehruvian model in the world's most plural society and the world's largest democracy of a billion, find more realistic and less expensive roles for more effective law and order for its citizens, be a fair regulator, not a provider of all economic activities, and be a prudent *grihast*, not a profligate squanderer of a poor nation's resources and end public loot for private fortunes with less controls? How to grow out of the pigmy role of a 0.5 per cent economy in the global market? At the heart of India's economic and security problem is the political leadership of straw and cardboard, which cannot make a strong, viable, sustainable state. The basic logic is as follows. If India needs a bottom-line of a 7 per cent p.a. rate of economic growth to abolish poverty, to give more employment, and to generate resources for security, infrastructure, social development, and exports — at the past capital-output ratio of 4:1 — it must have a savings rate of atleast 28 per cent p.a. Not only has this never been achieved, it has recently sunk to below 20 per cent, because of governments' profligacy and finan-cial mismanagement, and because the political leadership has feather-bedded itself and less than 20 million white and blue collared people in the state sector, with the molly-coddling of a controlled, non-competitive economy. So government, the largest spender, the biggest drain on GNP, not only cannot contribute to savings, but also by bloating its inefficient apparatus, has burdened India with non-serviceable debts, growing very fast. A debt trap and a national savings rate of 28 per cent can hardly go together, in these circumstances. That is the nub of the problem; the details have been indicated in the preceding chapters. There is no scope left for cheap populism. That zero-sum game has been played to its limit. If the fundamentals of economic, foreign and international trade, energy, and technology policies have gone wrong, and beyond the capacity of the polity to change; then those policies and that polity has to change for India to survive.

Lastly, how can we ensure better self-correcting mechanisms?

— With more transparency and public accountability.

— With more responsible legislative functioning, scrutiny and accountability of the Executive through effective committees.

— Through a free investigative media, English and vernacular.

— Through an independent and efficient judiciary in the higher and lower courts.

— A more responsive, more honest governing Executive.

All this really means a new social contract for the next fifty years between the governments and people of India. In these last fifty years the Indian mind, contrary to Tagore's fervent prayer, has not 'lead us forward into ever widening thought and action'; but into ever-narrowing *galis* of divisiveness, ambition, greed, distrust, and violence, ending with international insignificance for a country of a billion intelligent, enterprising people. This has been the product of that 'spastic' state. The end of the road of forces in 'closed systems' (in Indian atavism in internal and foreign policies) is entropy; a running down and a collapse of systems. Insular closed minds, not those of Tagore's 'ever-widening thought and action', have been at the root of Indian atavism, leading to the atrophy and decline of most institutions, damaging nation-building.

At last, the nation's ultimate bane. Ambivalence is the hallmark of Indians in and out of government and politics. It is a social malaise which retards progress and all that a planning society ostensibly desires to achieve. Since Gandhi, we have wanted to be a free people, but we also want to inherit the authoritarian style of the family *karta*, the landlord, the raja, and even the *swami*! So we readily took over the authoritarian legislation and imperialistic trappings of our earlier British masters. We want good impartial government, but we also want to get every personal advantage from the system, without any objection, discipline, or sense of public interest. We want social justice, but we will not change our social attitudes to caste and class inequalities, exercising the basic desire to dominate, rather than empower, delegate, and get objective accountability for performance. Instead of objectivity in government, and dissent in a democracy, Mrs Indira Gandhi epitomised the ethos by demanding personal 'commitment'. We boast of the Rule of Law, and try to get around every law, if not brazenly violate it, not excluding the law-makers, who would like to believe that they are above the law, and dislike 'judicial activism'. We plug the mother tongue in our politics, but the ruling classes send their children to English medium schools. The ruling classes decry western culture, but their first desire is to send their children to the West for higher education and dollar incomes. That same culture is hardly exhibited in the best *dharmic* relations with each other in politics, work, business, and neighbourhood. We want a planned economy, but we refuse to discard inefficiencies in work, low productivity with bloated uneconomic employment, a poor work ethic, besides not being result-oriented.

What then is planning for? To provide a vast *jajmani* (patron-client) network of public expenditures for ostensible development and poverty alleviation; but really for private loot by those in power. We wish to remove poverty, but the bulk of public expenditures and subsidies do not even reach the poor. We regard the care of the Environment as a 'sacred' obligation to a past forest-based civilisation, producing the Epics, Vedanta and Upanishad; but we do not hesitate to decimate forests for revenue, private gain, and political funds, pollute even the Ganga, and make Delhi's air unbreatheable. Lastly, we talk a lot, dispute endlessly, and achieve too little too late. This widespread ambivalence has to be cured, if we want India to be democratic, well governed, more achieving, a player on the world stage befitting India's long unrealised potential.

That, Mr. Deve Gowda, is what went wrong, in the heart and the limbs of the Indian state and society. In response to this question at the end of the twentieth century, one must turn to another simple question posed by Lenin in 1904, at the beginning of the century: 'What Is To Be Done?' That is for you and your political generation of leaders in power to decide — if you wish to avoid the dust-bin of history, which awaits all failures, and when, as Shakespeare wrote, they are 'drest in a little brief authority', they even 'make the angels weep', not to speak of suffering humans.

I would like to end on this note of human suffering, so absent from political debate in and out of the legislatures by the self-proclaimed representatives of those suffering millions. Ideologies, policies, plans and statistics apart, how can the Indian people really know social justice, the aim of the Indian Constitution and its Five-Year Plans, the cry of poets and film-makers, the hollow claim of politicians, the vain boast of governments, without knowing social suffering in the heart? Yet no Plan, no politician speaks of that deceptive, silent suffering of mind, body and spirit of the poor and oppressed, especially women and children. In thirty-five years of visiting Parliament and reading its proceedings in the press, I know of only one call in its precincts to relieve human suffering, and that is by a non-politician in the Rajya Sabha for the child. It was when the writer, R.K. Narayan of Malgudi fame pleaded to relieve the load of books from little children's backs; which no politician has had eyes to see or feel. As I said earlier, no Bihar minister, in the halcyon first years of Nehru, still wearing Gandhi's khadi and cap, bothered to come and see the suffering of thousands of the poor, helpless, malaria-stricken victims of the Kosi floods in my three years.

Once an indignant Nehru plunged into communal rioters in Delhi in 1947; not to speak of Gandhi's bleeding heart on lone missions to Calcutta and Noakholi in the times of the long knives and communal madness. But where was Nehru's grandson, Rajiv, Congress ministers, and members of Parliament when, in three shameful days and nights, the Calcutta killings of 1946 were repeated on 3,000 helpless Sikh men, women and children in the capital city itself. A community, of which India could be proud, were shamelessly massacred by political bullies in their homes and in the streets of Delhi itself. The Japanese have since apologised for war-time crimes in East Asia. The ruling Congress party has not apologised for Delhi, 1984. Nor did most of the political class care. Where were political bleeding hearts in the disastrous Bhopal explosion, the worst human tragedy in industrial history? Or when millions have been uprooted from their ancestral lands and homes at dams and project sites, with callous 'resettlement'? Beyond the press, where was the political outcry against the Bhagalpur blindings; against fake police encounters killing non-culpable citizens; or thousands of men, women and children locked up without charge, trial or bail for indefinite periods? Have the law-makers and the police uprooted the slum mafia oppressing slum dwellers, or are they sharers of power and conduits for votes?

Political chauvinists are out to make a little political capital when two Kentucky Fried Chicken shops are opened. The same people have cared not a damn, when hundreds of millions have suffered from malnutrition; or millions do not get good and regular supplies of essential foodgrains, sugar and kerosene oil at thousands of shops in the public distribution system. The same ambivalent Indian chauvinists are indignant when Yanni comes to Agra to fulfil a life-long desire to play his music near the Taj Mahal, itself described as 'frozen music'. But none of these chauvinists' hearts are touched or laws enforced to relieve the endless suffering of poor Indian girls and women brutally raped ever so often; sent into the flesh trade because of poverty in the flower of their youth; and murdered for venal dowries in the outlaw culture of in-laws. Heartless ambivalence is widespread in all kinds of suffering.

Till we share and are moved by social suffering around us each day of our lives, social justice of the 'leaders' and the intellectuals will continue to be a hollow, heartless, political manipulation of the sufferers. Social justice as a political policy needs to be internalised first in the social conscience of political and intellectual leaders; and only then externalised in effective public measures beyond political manifesto and public policy. Or else they will continue to be what they are, public frauds on the manipulated poor, and an exhibition of false cultural ambivalence in vocal India.

The states of India and Pakistan were born in the savage pain of millions. The state has lived on as an icon in whose name cruelty and pain are widely afflicted through mindless institutionalisation of a power-mad ruling class, indifferent to human suffering. The state itself is indifferent to people's pain and suffering; sadly, even in state hospitals, schools and homes for women and the retarded. How can such a state even feel social injustice and human suffering? In '*Transactions in the Construction of Pain,*' (*Daedalus*, Winter, 1996) Veena Das herself wrote with pain: 'It worries me that I have been unable to name that which died when autonomous citizens of India were simultaneously born as monsters.' She added, 'Whilst those who found speech easily, as in the political debates of abducted women in the Constituent Assembly, continue to talk of national honour when dealing with violence that women have had to endure in every communal riot since the Partition.' This was after one hundred thousand women from both sides of the border were forcibly abducted and raped. Earlier she wrote with deep insight: 'The everyday life embodied in tradition lives as much in the worship of icons (the husband is god), as the new trasnformations that Sandip (a character in Tagore's '*Ghose Boire*') is trying to bring (nation as god)'.

As an ex-historian I believe that nothing died when Veena Das' 'autonomous citizens of India were simultaneously born as monsters'. That something only lay dormant during the reforming transition and effective government of the British raj. It was reversion to the cultural psyche of a long past, a reversion which itself deserves a book by a social psychologist like Sudhir Kakar. After all, Africa is returning to a tribal past. And behind the modern apparatus of a communist state, Mao's China has has reverted, in spirit, to the days of Celestial Empire. So behind the facade of modernisation, much in India in these last fifty years has been a characteristic reversion to an atavistic past, too complex to explain here.

Hence, my plea for a second liberation movement from the worst in that past which will be far more difficult, and far more prolonged than liberation from the British. To save ourselves from ourselves should be the new *dharma*.

A Postcript

This book was written at the end of 1996. Before the manuscript goes to print in May 1997, the publishers have asked me if I would care to consider any recent developments of significance. Perhaps, there are only two; the rest of the polity remains in the same serpentine coils as in the past.

The first is the real testing time in recent past for a coalition government which truly represents the political assertion of the world's most pluralist society, in a way no previous Indian government has known. That coalition represents Centre and Left parties, caste, linguistic and regional groups. It represents a marked shift of power to states and regional parties, and a compulsion of more Federal governance. And, for the third time in a decade, the defeated Congress party — once itself a coalition formation from the freedom struggle years — is lending and again withdrawing its support abruptly; for reasons not clearly and credibly given to the people of India, or even to the party itself. It looks like a gamble for power by one man, acting President of a party which has itself lost inner democracy and respect for the people of India. The situation was summed up in the heading of a *London Times* article of 14.4.97: India's Nadir: The Country teeters as the Congress Party rots.' So India has to learn the realities of frame working, stable coalitions; or be written off as a future player in a globalising competitive world. If it fails, that plurality will show up an unchanging anthropological relic of long past history, though a fraction of it may dress up in the garb of the twentieth century.

The second is the Chidambaram budget, a remarkable performance of a thirteen-party coalition of such diverse views, and a significant second step after Dr. Manmohan Singh's post-1991 budgets, leading India towards a more competitive liberalised economy. More than any other past budget, it was an expression of faith in Indian tax-payers, Indian industry and Indian exporters after the typical dithering since 1993-94 of the Rao government. It promised to be a new base of higher growth, the generation of higher revenues for larger investment in the crumbling infrastructure, and the long-deprived social development sector in health, family planning and education; with reasonable control on inflation and fiscal deficits. No budget of the past elicited such widespread confidence across the political and economic spectrum. It had a refreshing new vision of India as a future competitive Asian player. The Kesri Congress' adventurist bid for power — and to save its skin from accumulating 'judicial activism' for its past sins — has done more than put that promising budget on the back-burner for the present. Its fate is uncertain at the time of writing. The President, the Lok Sabha Speaker and political good sense may save it.

If ever there was a contrast between the interests of the Congress party and the interests of the people of India and India's international image; it has been in the recent exhibition of Kesri's private brinkmanship. It hit that landmark budget in its infancy, though it was acclaimed nationally and internationally; and the government of India lives precariously on a vote on account expiring in a month. It came at the time of the Non-aligned Conference in New Delhi, with the presence of the new UN Secretary-General. It came at a time of renewed Indo-Pakistan talks with more hope then in many past years. It came at a time when the truckers carrying 60 per cent of India's goods, went on strike, hitting millions in the markets, involving the economy in losses of thousands of crores a day, and causing infinite suffering to poor millions facing scarcity and still higher prices which have shot up from 25 per cent to 100 per cent. It came at a time of a food policy and an energy pricing crises and changes in Import-Export policies; all vital national issues. But Kesri and his crew could not care less. The human suffering of millions did not touch them. Was this the politics of a leader from the violent *lathi* and *bhais* backwoods of the middle Gangetic plain, holding the country to ransom for purely personal ends? If so, the next election may bring the final retribution to this slow-dying party, emasciated by in-fighting and corruption, indifferent to the nation, forgetting the higher Nehru tradition, and afraid to face the electorate. For the moment, India's progress is halted, its credibility abroad damaged, its government stalled. Selfish politicians hold India by its throat. We are reverting to Rajaji's historical statement that

India was "a governmentless society". We are witnessing the last phase of the pale Bahadur Shahs since Nehru's times, with the power to wound the nation, not govern it wisely. India needs a new liberation struggle from those evils, from those obsolete minds, led by a new generation of leaders of real substance, a national and international vision, and a modicum of conscience; themselves liberated from the worst in India's past retarding coils.

But that will not be easy. Those long historic coils go deep and far back; to the Vedas which, despite their high mindedness, also nurtured a singular self-righteous isolation from the rest of the world 'between the northern mountains and the southern seas'. That was not the fault of the Vedas, which were outstanding works of their time, but of unchanging minds since. They go back to Chanakya and the state's powerful patronising, controlling role amidst widespread corruption and spying for internal rather than external security; to Manu and the concretising of divisive caste as the world's most unchanging social system; to Aurangzeb and Shivaji, and the psycho-social roots of Hindu-Muslim communalism; to a feudal landlord culture exploiting caste, land and water resources. Many Indians seem to have an 'unfinished business' with Ghazni, Ghori, and the Mughals, on the one hand; and with the East India Company, on the other. They go forward in the rear-view mirror of time. India still carries this heavy atavistic load of the past. Now with the world's largest numbers of poor, illiterates, and malnourished women and children, it is the worst legacy of the misrule of politicians in the last fifty years. So the second liberation movement has to be a movement for the freedom of minds from the serpentine coils of that deeply embedded atavism. It is an old bed of snakes, which the first generation of freedom fighters failed to see in their unhistorical idealism. Superficial pink socialism could hardly blend with this archaic, feudal heritage of state and society. The latter swallowed pink solidism like a python roused in long sleep. Atavism has, in these fifty years, asserted itself above both earlier idealism and later realism, from village landlord to government minister. Indian plurality is in danger of being atomised by narrow self-seeking politicians from such an intensely plural society which knows no clear directions, and lacks clear political will.

When and how will we see that second liberation movement, an internalised revolution of minds, society, and governance? That is essential for the inevitable coalitions of India's most plural society to be durable and forward-looking, and purposeful as East Asia.

Index